UNIVERSITY OF CINCINNATI
CLASSICAL STUDIES
IV

STUDIES IN FIFTH-CENTURY ATTIC EPIGRAPHY

Studies in Fifth-Century Attic Epigraphy

By
Donald William Bradeen
Malcolm Francis McGregor

Published by the University of Oklahoma Press, Norman, for the University of Cincinnati

Library of Congress Cataloging in Publication Data

Bradeen, Donald William, 1918–1973.
Studies in fifth-century Attic epigraphy.

Bibliography: p. 131
1. Inscriptions, Greek—Athens. I. McGregor, Malcolm Francis, 1910– joint author. II. Title.
CN384.B7 481'.7 72-9258
ISBN 0-8061-1064-3

Preface

When we arranged to spend the academic year 1967–68 in Athens, our intention was to examine the lettering of all the public documents of the fifth century B.C. in the hope of establishing firm criteria for dating. Our plans were well advanced when Russell Meiggs's important study of letter-forms, concentrating on the period 460–430 B.C., appeared in *J.H.S.*, LXXXVI (1966), pp. 86–98. We decided to persist, in order to test the conclusions reached by Meiggs and to extend the area of study to cover the century to the end of the Peloponnesian War.

We soon became aware that to adhere unwaveringly to a single project in the Epigraphic Museum requires more intellectual strength than we possess. At frequent intervals our curiosity was stimulated by the observation that the published record does not reproduce the truth about a given document or group of fragments. In these cases we did not resist the temptation to conduct thorough examinations.

The acknowledgement of our responsibility to place before our epigraphic colleagues the results of these studies has led us to the writing of this book, in which, on the basis of what we regard as careful scrutiny of the stones, we expound our views about a number of inscriptions that have been the subject of interesting controversy.

The reader will soon note that our practice in regard to restoration, that much debated issue, has not been wholly consistent. In Chapters III–VII we have been reasonably conservative, placing our trust in square brackets to indicate what was probably inscribed by the mason and inserting in the commentary what might have been. The Regulations for Miletos (Chapter II) posed a special problem. The text was a long one and much of it is now lost. We did develop a conception of the regulations laid down by the Athenians and how these might have been expressed. Yet we hesitated to place such extensive restoration in the text, even with the protection of square brackets. The commentary, naturally, became long, and we could scarcely expect a reader to reconstruct a possible continuous text from it. We have therefore printed two texts, the first embracing restorations that we consider all but sure, the second a version that shows how our interpretations might have been phrased. Our second text is an example of what S. Dow has called "the principle of extreme freedom"; *Conventions in Editing*, pp. 22–23.

Quota-list 26, in Chapter I, is an exception to our policy of caution. The obverse surface of the stone is, for the most part, either smooth or discouragingly eroded, and here, if we have erred, we have erred on the side of daring.

That a new edition of *Inscriptiones Graecae*, I, has been in preparation is well known. We have seized the opportunity of conscientiously re-examining every text for which B. D. Meritt and M. F. McGregor, D. W. Bradeen, and A. G. Woodhead are responsible.

Our studies in Athens taught us much. In particular, we learned once again the lesson that in epigraphical study there is no substitute for autopsy. The photograph and, especially, the squeeze are indispensable and make "arm-chair" epigraphy a profitable exercise. The stone itself, however, is the final witness. This was brought home to us vividly by our inspection of documents that were the subject of study in those tragic years when Athens was inaccessible to scholars.

These relevant diversions were a factor in our inability to have completed, as yet, our announced project, the establishing of firm criteria, based on letter-forms, for the dating of fifth-century public documents. Nevertheless, we made substantial progress, and it is worth recording that we found no evidence whatever that impugns the validity of Meiggs's conclusions. In other words, the "orthodox" creed must still be accepted and, so far as we are concerned, the three-barred sigma alone serves as a divisional point chronologically at about 446 B.C.

We have many debts to acknowledge for the rare good fortune of spending the academic year 1967–68 in Greece, chiefly in the Epigraphic Museum. Bradeen expresses his thanks to the University of Cincinnati for leave, to the American Council of Learned Societies for financial support, and to the American School of Classical Studies at Athens for his associate membership. McGregor is grateful to the University of British Columbia for leave and to its President's Research Fund for financial support, to The Canada Council, which appointed him to a Senior Fellowship, and to the American School of Classical Studies at Athens, where he held a Visiting Professorship. Both of us acknowledge the many kindnesses of Henry S. Robinson, Director of the School.

We cannot write too glowingly of the assistance given to us so unstintingly by Mrs. D. Peppas-Delmouzou, Director of the Epigraphic Museum, and her superbly skillful and sympathetic staff; working conditions in the Museum are ideal, and we here pay the warmest possible tribute to the Greek authorities.

Nor will mere words adequately repay what we owe to Donald R. Laing of Case Western Reserve University, who was ever ready to interrupt his own work in order to lend us his critical eye and judgment, his technical ingenuity, and his photographic experience. We also appreciate the frequent help we received from Michael B. Walbank, now of the University of Calgary, who, apart from other contributions, joined EM 5417 to *I.G.*, I^2, 68/69 and is equal author of Chapter IV.

The typing of an epigraphic manuscript is often complex. This one has been revised several times, and we have profited from the patience of Mrs. Donald Bradeen, Miss Jessie Field, and Mrs. Gordon Young.

Both of us benefited from the generosity of Louise Taft Semple in her lifetime. Now we feel a special sense of gratitude and pride in the fact that the Classics Fund established by her has made possible the publication of this book.

Donald W. Bradeen
University of Cincinnati

Malcolm Francis McGregor
University of British Columbia

January, 1973

Contents

	Preface	Page vii
	List of Plates	xiii
	List of Abbreviations	xv
I	The Attic Quota-List of 429/8 B.C.	3
II	Regulations for Miletos	24
III	The Alliance with Egesta	71
IV	Athens and the Boiotians (Written in collaboration with Michael Burke Walbank of the University of Calgary)	82
V	Athens and Kolophon	94
VI	The Proxeny-Decree *I.G.*, I^2, 149	100
VII	Adnotationes Epigraphicae	106
	Bibliography	131
	List of Inscriptions Cited and Studied	139

List of Plates

I	List 26, obverse surface, upper section	*page* 5
II	List 26, obverse surface, lower section	6
III	List 26, left lateral surface	7
IV	*I.G.*, I^2, 22 (D11), Regulations for Miletos, showing the relationship between the two upper fragments (*a* left, *b* right)	26
V	*I.G.*, I^2, 22 (D11), fragments *a*, *b*, and *c* (the lower fragment), illustrating the "shelf" created by the fractures of *b* and *c*	27
VI	*I.G.*, I^2, 22 (D11), the reconstructed stele	28
VII	*I.G.*, I^2, 22 (D11), fragment *a*	29
VIII	*I.G.*, I^2, 19, the Treaty with Egesta, upper fragment	73
IX	*I.G.*, I^2, 20, the Treaty with Egesta, lower fragment (top two lines)	74
X	*I.G.*, I^2, 68/69, Athens and the Boiotians, reconstructed stele (fragments 2–5)	84
XI	*I.G.*, I^2, 68/69, fragment 1, showing the molding	85
XII	*I.G.*, I^2, 68/69, fragment 4	86
XIII	*I.G.*, I^2, 68/69, fragment 5	87
XIV	EM 2376, now part of *I.G.*, I^2, 14/15 (D15), Athens and Kolophon	95

XV	*I.G.*, I², 149, showing the joins	*page* 101
XVI	*I.G.*, I², 29	107
XVII	*I.G.*, I², 34, fragments *a* and *b*	108
XVIII	*I.G.*, I², 35, lines 12–23 (reverse surface of *I.G.*, I², 34)	109
XIX	*I.G.*, I², 35, lines 1–11 (=*c*)	110
XX	*I.G.*, I², 52, the Treaty with Leontinoi	111
XXI	*I.G.*, I², 60, fragment *f*, now in the Musée du Louvre	112
XXII	*I.G.*, I², 60, the Treaty with Mytilene, as reconstructed	113
XXIII	*I.G.*, I², 87, the Treaty with Halieis, without the fragment now in Cambridge	114
XXIV	*I.G.*, I², 101	115

List of Abbreviations

A.F.D. Benjamin Dean Meritt, *Athenian Financial Documents of the Fifth Century*

A.J.A. *American Journal of Archaeology*

A.J.P. *American Journal of Philology*

A.S.&I. *Ancient Society and Institutions: Studies Presented to Victor Ehrenberg on His 75th Birthday*, ed. E. Badian (Oxford, 1966)

A.T.L. Benjamin Dean Meritt, H. T. Wade-Gery, Malcolm Francis McGregor, *The Athenian Tribute Lists*

Abh. Ak. Berlin *Abhandlungen der preussischen Akademie der Wissenschaften*, philosophisch-historische Klasse

Agora Inv. No. I This gives the inventory number of inscriptions found in the excavation of the Athenian Agora by the American School of Classical Studies at Athens

Ant. Hell. A. R. Rangabé, *Antiquités Helléniques*

Att. Urkund. Adolf Wilhelm, *Attische Urkunden*

B.C.H. *Bulletin de Correspondance Hellénique*

B.S.A. *The Annual of the British School at Athens*

BM This symbol identifies readings offered by D. W. Bradeen and M. F. McGregor

Class. Quart. *The Classical Quarterly*

Commentary A. W. Gomme (and A. Andrewes, K. J. Dover), *A Historical Commentary on Thucydides*

D.A.T. Benjamin Dean Meritt, *Documents on Athenian Tribute*

Δελτ. Ἀρχ. *Δελτίον Ἀρχαιολογικόν*

EM These letters refer to the inventory of inscriptions in the Epigraphical Museum at Athens

Ἐφ. Ἀρχ. *Ἐφημερὶς Ἀρχαιολογική*

G.H.I. Russell Meiggs, David Lewis, *A Selection of Greek Historical Inscriptions to the End of the Fifth Century B.C.*

G.H.I., I^2 Marcus N. Tod, *A Selection of Greek Historical Inscriptions to the End of the Fifth Century B.C.*, I, second edition

G.R.B.S. *Greek Roman and Byzantine Studies*

Gött. gel. Anz. *Göttingische gelehrte Anzeigen*

H.S.C.P. *Harvard Studies in Classical Philology*

Hiller see *I.G.*, I^2

I.G., I Adolph Kirchhoff (ed.), *Inscriptiones Graecae*, I, *Inscriptiones Atticae Euclidis anno vetustiores*

I.G., I^2 Friedrich Hiller von Gaertringen (ed.), *Inscriptiones Graecae*, I, *Inscriptiones Atticae Euclidis anno anteriores*, editio minor

I.G., II^2 Johannes Kirchner (ed.), *Inscriptiones Graecae*, II–III, *Inscriptiones Atticae Euclidis anno posteriores*, editio minor

I.G., V, 2 Friedrich Hiller von Gaertringen (ed.), *Inscriptiones Graecae*, V, 2, *Inscriptiones Arcadiae*

I.G., XII, 8 C. Fredrich (ed.), *Inscriptiones Graecae*, XII, 8, *Inscriptiones insularum maris Thracici*

I.G., XIV Georg Kaibel (ed.), *Inscriptiones Graecae*, XIV, *Inscriptiones Italiae et Siciliae*

J.H.S. *The Journal of Hellenic Studies*

Kirchhoff see *I.G.*, I

Klio *Klio, Beiträge zur alten Geschichte*

Meisterhans-Schwyzer K. Meisterhans, *Grammatik der attischen Inschriften*, third edition, edited by Eduard Schwyzer

Personennamen Friedrich Bechtel, *Die historischen Personennamen des Griechischen bis zur Kaiserzeit*

Rev. ét. anc. *Revues des études anciennes*

S.E.G. *Supplementum Epigraphicum Graecum*

Sitzungsb. Ak. München *Sitzungsberichte der philosophisch-philologischen und historischen Classe der k.b. Akademie der Wissenschaften zu München*

Sitzungsb. Ak. Wien *Sitzungsberichte der Akademie der Wissenschaften in Wien*, philosophisch-historische Klasse

T.A.P.A. *Transactions of the American Philological Association*

STUDIES IN FIFTH-CENTURY ATTIC EPIGRAPHY

CHAPTER I

The Attic Quota-List of 429/8 B.C.

(Plates I–III)

Our curiosity about the quota-list numbered 26 and dated in 429/8 B.C. by B. D. Meritt, H. T. Wade-Gery, and M. F. McGregor[1] was aroused by H. B. Mattingly's effort[2] to place the list in 427/6 B.C. and by scepticism concerning the reading [Θ]ερ[αῖ]οι in 26, III, 23. Our initial inspection of the stone was undertaken in the hope that we could wring from the prescript evidence to establish a specific date securely. We became convinced that a minutely comprehensive examination would yield new readings and justify the time expended;[3] ultimately, we devoted six consecutive weeks to this stele, to say nothing of frequent later returns.[4]

[1] *The Athenian Tribute Lists*, I and II (1939 and 1949), List 26. Bibliography and epigraphic commentary will be found in I, pp. 93, 95–96; the text on p. 150; general bibliography and commentary on pp. 195–96. The text is reproduced in II, p. 30. For further bibliography see *S.E.G.*, X, 171; XIX, 21; XXI, 63. The reverse and left lateral faces may be observed in the foreground of Fig. 2 in *A.T.L.*, I, p. 5; the left lateral surface is legible in Fig. 127 on p. 95; a photograph of the obverse side serves as the frontispiece of *A.T.L.*, IV (1953). We publish our own photographs in Plates I–III. We collate by the text of *A.T.L.*, II.

[2] *Historia*, X (1961), pp. 166–68; *Class. Quart.*, N.S. XI (1961), pp. 154–65; XVI (1966), pp. 179–83; *B.S.A.*, LXV (1970), pp. 129–49.

[3] This is not to deny that the stone was read carefully by our predecessors. Nevertheless, we have learned much in the past generation, and technique has improved. Moreover, we suspect that, thanks largely to the advice of Donald R. Laing, we were able to isolate each *stoichos* with greater accuracy than has hitherto been attained.

[4] We have acknowledged our many debts in the Preface. Here we pay special tribute to our colleague Donald R. Laing, whose ingenuity enabled us to scrutinize

Our text of this list depends on three fragments of Pentelic marble, one of which, a small sliver from the left lateral surface, was seen only by Pittakys. The surviving two have been joined in the Epigraphical Museum to produce a stele at least 1.59 m. high (top and probably bottom are preserved), 0.824 m. wide (both sides are preserved), and 0.178 m. thick (at col. I, 13). The back of the stele is smooth, with a sag in the middle; the right edge is rounded. Hence the original thickness must be computed; we make it *ca* 0.184 m. (at col. I, 13). Across the top and for a distance of *ca* 0.195 m. down the left side of the reverse a belt of marble has been gouged out to a maximum depth of *ca* 0.056 m.[5]

The catalogue in *A.T.L.*, I (pp. 93, 95–96) supplies commentary on three extant fragments. In fact there are only two, now joined and carrying the same inventory number (EM 6856) in the Epigraphic Museum; how the error arose we cannot say, nor is it important.[6] Fragment 1 bears on its obverse face the prescript and II, 6–37, III, 6–37 (numeral-column), and IV, 6–24; fragment 3 has II, 37–56, III, 37–59, and IV, 24–58; fragment 2, now lost, broke away from the left lateral surface of fragment 1, which contains col. I.

The entries below the prescript on the obverse face were cut in three columns; the left lateral surface, despite the fact that as a convenience to the reader's eye its contents are labeled col. I in *A.T.L.*, I and II, was the last to be utilized, as an appendix. The lettering and orthography are Attic, except that in col. I, which is inscribed by a second hand, eta is engraved in lines 6, 13, and 21. The chequer-pattern (excluding the prescript) is, so far as it can be measured, 0.016 m. in height by

with confidence a badly eroded stone letter-space by letter-space, and whose critical eye and judgment often saved us from error and reinforced our patience.

[5] See the photograph in *A.T.L.*, I, p. 5. O. Broneer, *Hesperia*, IV (1935), pp. 157–58, suggested that *A.T.L.*, II, List 35 and the lower fragments of List 39 might have broken away from this area. Our computation of the original thickness of the stele, however, argues against this; the smaller fragments are too thick to fit.

[6] So far as we can determine, three extant fragments are first mentioned in *A.T.L.*, I.

Plate I. List 26, obverse surface, upper section (*Photograph courtesy of the National Epigraphic Museum*)

Plate II. List 26, obverse surface, lower section (*Photograph courtesy of the National Epigraphic Museum*)

Plate III. List 26, left lateral surface (*Photograph courtesy of the National Epigraphic Museum*)

ca 0.013 m. in width (but there is much variation in cols. III and IV).

The obverse surface of this stele is in appalling condition and, to judge from his report, has been since at least the time of Rangabé (1842).[7] Much of the stone is worn, eroded, and scarred; the upper section, however, where the prescript must be sought, is smooth, and in the right-hand corner the letters are comparatively easy to read (especially the demotics of lines 1 and 2). Significantly, they reveal the rust-colored patina that so often settles in letters engraved in Pentelic marble. Elsewhere on the stele there remain traces of this patina where the actual cut of the chisel cannot be detected. We believe that these traces frequently represent all that survives of letters and have accordingly made what seem to us the appropriate identifications. Sometimes, of course, marks of the chisel may be recognized along with the patina.

We emphasize the difficulties encountered in the examination of the stele. Over many weeks, during which we became intimately familiar with this formidable stone, we found that a letter could be read credibly in one light but not at all in another. The experienced epigraphist knows that very often the brightest light, *e.g.*, the mid-day sunlight of Hellas, is not best for extracting the maximum possible from a damaged surface. We welcome those who will collate our text against the stone, but we urge them to be persistent, to return time and again.

So far as we can tell, of the early editors Rangabé, Pittakys, and Köhler saw the two extant fragments. On the basis of a collation of their texts, we do not believe that, in nearly a century and a half, the condition of the surfaces has changed significantly. In other words, our assumption is that we should

[7] *Antiquités Helleniques*, I, nos. 223, 224. It was for this reason that no photograph was published in *A.T.L.*, I. In response to queries the authors presented a photograph in *A.T.L.*, IV; the reader is invited to inspect this and our own photographs in Plates I–III.

be able to identify the readings of previous editors. Since we cannot always do this, we have in many cases discarded readings claimed or accepted by our predecessors, which will account for some of the differences between our text and that of *A.T.L.*, II. In this respect we have subscribed to orthodox epigraphic conservatism. In another respect we have not been conservative. We hope that we shall not be considered arrogant in asserting that we have reclaimed, with our own eyes, the maximum from the physical evidence, at least under present conditions and with the techniques now known.

We set out our revised text below. The deterioration of the stone since ancient times and the hazards of reading have led us to write a more detailed epigraphic commentary than is customary.

COMMENTARY

Line 1: In what must be the third *stoichos* (see on line 4 below) the vertical cutting is the iota of [ἐπ]ί̣. The three upper strokes of sigma are visible, but not in bright light, in the twelfth *stoichos*. Of the alpha of [κ]α̣[ί], the crossbar and the lower half of the right diagonal are missing. Three spaces further on the lower half of what must be iota is legible (cutting). The chisel has left its traces of all strokes of the word's final sigma; the fourth (lowest) stroke, roughly parallel to the second, is also marked by a touch of color. Most of the two letters read in ἀ̣[ρχ]ệ[ς] survive (cutting). Few traces of the relative pronoun (the upper right tip of the *daseia*, the top of iota) are clearly incised but the rough scars in the marble form the expected shapes and we withhold dots. The delta of the proper name is an elusive letter; it is a comparatively broad impression, almost an abrasion, properly shaped and placed, satisfyingly visible in some lights but not at all in others.[8]

[8] We are tempted to advise the reader to challenge the stone in the half-light of a winter's mid-morning and to dispense with the electric light.

ΣΤΟΙΧ. 47

[Ἐπ]ὶ̣[τêς hέκτε]ς[κ]α̣[ὶ ε]ἰ̣[κοστê]ς ἀ[ρχ]ê[ς]hêι Δ[ά]μ̣ιππος Φυλάσιος
[ἐγραμμάτευε hελλενοταμία]ι̣ ἐ̂[σα]ν Θ̣εό̣δορος̣ Ἀναγυράσιος
[. . .]ε̣[. . .]ς̣[. . . . . 33 . . . .]ος Σφέτ
τ[ιος . . . . 38 . . . .]Ἐπικρ̣
[άτες – – – – – – – – – – – – – – – –]

II [Θράικιος]		III [Νεσιοτικός]		IV [Ἰονικός]	
– – – – –	– – – – –	– – – – –	– – – – –	– – – – –	– – – – –
– – – – –	[Θραμβ]α[ῖ]οι	– – – – –	– – – – –	– – – – –	– – – – –
ΔΓ⊢IIII	Ἀργί[λιοι]	– – – – –	– – – – –	– – – – –	[Βρυκôς Κ]αρπάθο
ΔΓ⊢II[II]	Στ̣[α]γ[ιρîται]	– – – – –	– – – – –	– – – – –	[Βρυκôς] π̣ε[ρ]υσινô
HHH	[Ἀφ]υτα[îοι]	– – – – –	– – – – –	– – – – –	– – – – –
𐅅HHHH	Σκιοναî[ο]ι	– – – – –	– – – – –	[. . . .]Γ[– – –]	– – – – –
HHH	Ἀκάνθιο[ι]	– – – – –	ι̣[– – – – – –]	– – – – –	[Βρικινδά]ριοι
𐅅HHH	Μενδαîοι	– – – – –	– – – – –	[H]	[Μύρινα πα]ρὰ Κύμεν
[𐅄]	Νεοπολîται	HH	[Τένιοι]	[H𐅄ΔΓ⊢IIII]	[hαλικαρν]α̣σσιοι
	Μενδαίον	ΔΓ⊢II[II]	[Γρυνχêς]	– – – – –	[. . . ⁸ . . . .]ο̣ι
X]XX	Θάσιοι	𐅅H	Ἄ[νδριοι]	– – – – –	– – – – –
[ΔΔ]Γ	Ἴκιοι	HHḤ	[Χ]α̣[λκιδêς]	– – – – –	– – – – –
[ΔΓ]⊢̣IIII	Ν̣εοπολîται	Ḥ	Σερί[φιοι]	[Γ⊢⊢⊢II]	[Διοσερîτ]αι
	π̣[α]ρ' Ἀντισά[ρ]αν	Ḥ	Νισύ[ριοι]	– – – – –	– – – – –
[ΔΓ]⊢̣IIII	Γ̣[α]λέφσιοι	H	[Σ]τ[υ]ρê[ς]	[ΔΓ⊢IIII]	[Ἐλαιέα πα]ρὰ Μύρινα̣[ν]
[H]	Δ̣ιês ἐχς Ἄθο	ΔΔΓ	Σύριοι	– – – – –	[. . . . ¹⁰ . . . .]ς
– – – – –	[Αἰ]γάντιοι	HHH	[Θ]ερ[α]îοι	– – – – –	– – – – –
[ΔΓ⊢IIII]	Αἰνεâται	HΔΔΔ⊢̣⊢̣[II]	[Δι]ά̣[κριοι] ἐν [Εὐβοίαι]	– – – – –	– – – – –
[H]	Θ̣[ύ]σσιοι	𐅄	[Ἴ]ệ[ται]	– – – – –	– – – – –
[ΔΔΔ⊢]⊢̣⊢II	Ὀ̣[λ]ο̣φύχσιοι	HHH	– – – – –	– – – – –	– – – – –
[ΔΓ⊢II]I[I]	Σαναîοι	– – – – –	– – – – –	– – – – –	– – – – –
[HHH]	[Μ]α̣ρονîται	– – – – –	– – – – –	– – – – –	– – – – –
[XHH]	[Το]ρο[ν]αîοι	h[ε]λλε[σ]πόντιο[ς]		– – – – –	– – – – –
[X]	h[α]βδερîτ[α]ι	HH𐅄ΔΔΔΓ⊢⊢⊢̣	[Τ]ε[ν]έδ̣ι̣οι	– – – – –	– – – – –
[HH] ·	[Σα]μο[θρ]ᾳ̂ι̣[κ]ες	𐅅HHHΔΔΓ⊢̣⊢̣[⊢]	[Κ]υζ̣ι̣κε̣[νοί]	– – – – –	– – – – –
– – – – –	[Βεργ]αîοι	ḤHḤ	[Πρ]οκ̣[οννέσιοι]	– – – – –	– – – – –
– – – – –	– – – – –	𐅄̣𐅄ΔΔΔΓ	Χα̣λ̣[χεδόνιοι]	[ΔΔΔ⊢⊢⊢II]	[Κρυês ἀπὸ Καρία]ς
[ταîσδε ἔταχσαν h]οι		ΔΔΔ⊢̣⊢̣[⊢II]	Ἀρ̣τ̣[ακενοί]	– – – – –	– – – – –
[τάκται ἐπὶ Κρ. . .ο]		ḤΔ[ΔΔ]Γ⊢	[Λαμφσακενοί]	[𐅄]	[Θερμαîοι ἐχς Ἰ]κά[ρο]
[γραμματεύοντος]		Γ	hα[ρπαγιανοί]	[Γ⊢⊢⊢II]	[Αὐλιâται Κâρ]ε[ς]
[ΔΓ⊢IIII]	[Καλλιπολîται]	[Γ⊢⊢]⊢̣Ị[I]	[Δασκύλει]ον̣	[Γ⊢⊢⊢II]	[Μύνδιοι παρὰ] Τ[έρμ(ερα)]

[ΔΔΓ]	[Σαρταῖοι]	------------	[. .]α[.]ο[--]	[ΔΓ⊢IIII]	[Β]ọ[υθειε͂]ς
[ΔΓ⊢IIII]	[Κάσι]ο[ι]	[ΔΓ⊢I]I[II]	[Σιγ]ει̣[ε͂ς]	[ΔΓ⊢IIII]	[Καρβασυανδ]ε͂ς
[ΔΓ⊢III]I	Π̣[λ]ε[υμ]ε͂ς	------------	------------	[ΔΔΔ⊢⊢⊢II]	[Χαλ]κ[ει]ᾶ̣ται
[Η]	Ἀ̣[μ]ό[ργ]ι[οι]	------------	[. .]υ[----]	------------	------------
[Γ⊢⊢⊢II]	Αἰ̣ο[λῖ]τ[α]ι̣	------------	------------	------------	[. . ⁵⁻⁶ . .]ε[---]
[ταῖσδε βο]λὲ̣ [σὺν τ]ο͂ι		------------	------------	------------	------------
[δικαστερί]οι [ἔ]τα̣[χσεν]		------------	------------	[Η]	[h]αιρ[αι]ε͂ς
[ΔΔΔ]	Συμαῖοι	------------	------------	[Η]	[hα]ιρ[α]ιε͂[ς] περυσι[ν]ο͂
[Δ⊢⊢⊢II]	Δι̣α̣κρε͂[ς ἀ]π̣ὸ	------------	------------	[ΔΔΔ⊢̣⊢⊢II]	[Μαρ]αθέ̣σιọι̣
	Χαλ̣κ̣ιδ[έον]	------------	------------	------------	------------
[𐅄]	Β̣[υσβ]ι[κεν]ọ[ί]	------------	------------	[Η]	[Συαγγελε͂ς]
[Γ⊢⊢⊢II]	Κ̣[λε]ον[αί]	[⊢II]	[Μα]δ̣[ύ]τ̣[ιοι]		[hο͂ν ἄρχε]ι̣ [Πί]τ[ρες]
	vacat	------------	------------	------------	[. . . ⁷ . . .]οι
[hαί]δε τõν π[ό]λε[ο]ν [α]ὐτὲ[ν]		[ΔΔΔΓ⊢⊢]	Παρια[νοί]	------------	------------
τὲν ἀπα[ρ]χὲν ἀπέγαγον			Χερρονε[σῖται]	[ΗΗΗ]	[Χερρονέ]σ[ιο]ι
ΗΗΗ	Μεθον[α]ῖοι	------------	ἀπ' Ἀγο[ρᾶς]	------------	------------
ΔΓ⊢IIII	Α[ἰ]σόνιοι	------------	------------	------------	------------
Η	Δικαιοπολῖται	[⊢II]	[Ἀλοπ]ε[κοννέσιοι]	------------	------------
	Ἐρετριõν	[ΔΓ⊢⊢⊢]	[Ἐλαιόσι]ο[ι]	------------	------------
	vacat		[ἐν Χερρ]ο[νέσ]οι	[Η]	Ọ[ἰναῖο]ι [ἐχς Ἰ]κ̣[άρο]
		[Γ⊢⊢⊢II]	[Παλαιπερκόσ]ιο[ι]		*vacat?*
		[ΧΗΗ]Η̣Δ[---]	[Βυζάντιοι]		
			vacat?		

I

[hελ]λεσπόντ[ιος]

[ΔΓ]	Χαλχεδόν[ιοι]
[.ΔΔ]Δ⊢	Δαρδανε͂ς
[ΧΔ]ΔΔΓ	Λαμφσακεν[οί]
Χ̣𐅄ΗΗ⊢III	Βυζάντιοι
[. .]ỊỊ	Ἀβυδηνοί
[𐅄Δ]⊢̣⊢⊢	Παριανοί
[ΔΔ]Δ⊢̣⊢	Μαδύτιο[ι]
[Δ]ΔΔ⊢⊢	Ἐλ[α]ιόσι[οι]
[𐅄]ΔΔ⊢⊢	Κυζικενοί
[π]όλες αἵ[δ]ε ἀρχαῖς	
[ἔδ]οσαν τὸμ φόρον	
[. .]I	Λιμναῖοι [ἐ]ν Χερρονήσο[ι]
[.] *vac.*	Χερρο[ν]εσῖται ἀπ' Ἀγορᾶς
[h]αίδε π[ό]λες κατα-	
[δ]ελõσι τὸμ φόρον	
vacat	
[. .] *vac.*	Μυριναῖοι
[. . .] *vac.*	Ἴμβριοι
[Δ]Γ⊢IIII	Σέστιοι
[Δ]ΔΔ⊢⊢	Ἀλοπο[κ]οννήσιο[ι]
vacat	

Line 2: We add a dot to Meritt's iota;[9] we see the lower half. To the verb we supply the initial epsilon (we see all but the lowest horizontal) and we confirm Meritt's nu (the diagonal is convincing, the other strokes are best read in murky light); the alpha we cannot identify. In the proper name we remove the dot from epsilon (all horizontals are legible) and add a dot to sigma, of which we perceive only the upper angle. For the same reason we dot gamma in the demotic.

Line 3: We add the isolated epsilon (the vertical and the top horizontal) and sigma (perhaps the three upper strokes).

Line 4: The most important addition to the prescript is the tau, of which we are quite sure. Since it must be the second tau of *Σφέττιος*, it is therefore the first letter of the line; consequently we determine the length of line as 47 letters,[10] which restricts the restoration of the numeral in line 1 to [*hέκτε*]*ς*, [*ὀγδόε*]*ς*, or [*ἐνάτε*]*ς*. The years 430/29 and 428/7 are thus excluded as the date of this list. We regret that we can see no more of the numeral in line 1; thus we cannot on epigraphic grounds alone assert a specific date. We argue below, on other grounds, for 429/8 B.C.

COLUMN II

The reader will observe a number of minor discrepancies between our text and those of predecessors. We comment specifically only on those of some substance.

Line 10: Of sigma we read the top stroke, of tau the right half of the horizontal, of gamma the left side (color and

[9] *Documents on Athenian Tribute* (1937), pp. 99–100.

[10] We thus agree with Meritt's computation, *D.A.T.*, pp. 98–100. We reach 0.824 m. for the width of the stone. The margin on the left is greater (from the edge to the middle of the tau in line 4 = 0.031 m.) than that on the right (from the edge to the middle of the tau in line 3 = 0.021 m.). The distance of 0.772 m. from center to center of first and last letters produces, mathematically, somewhat more than 47 letters but not 48; we average the width of the *stoichos* as 0.0165 m. (Meritt made it 0.0169 m.) on the basis of the legible demotics in lines 1 and 2. There is no crowding as the eye moves left; rather, there seems to be a little slackening (measurement, of course, is perilous).

cutting) and the lower right. There is a suggestion of rho in an oval-shaped hollow.

Line 34: The final letter, we think, is iota; nu is much less probable. The vertical stroke projects up beyond the adjacent omicron, as iota does elsewhere on this stone when it has omicron as its neighbor; nu does not.[11] The restorations here and in lines 43–44 depend in part on our understanding of the dates and the relationship of Lists 25 and 26; see below, pp. 20–23.

Line 43: Only the vertical of epsilon is visible.

Line 44: A convincing iota follows omicron. Little (part of the horizontal) of tau remains but the left side and the joining crossbar of alpha make a dot unnecessary.

Line 51: Rangabé (*Ant. Hell.*, I, no. 224), followed by Pittakys (*'Εφ. Ἀρχ.* [1853], no. 1254), reads ΑΙΔΕ over ΤΕΝΑ. We see nothing before delta, of which the placing, immediately over Α, proves that the word was spelled with the *daseia*.[12]

COLUMN III

Line 13: The numeral 𐅅 printed in *A.T.L.* comes from Köhler.[13] We doubt if he saw it and suspect an editorial error in his plate. The vertical of the first letter is the upper half, on the left side of the *stoichos*.

Line 18: We have little confidence in the alpha; perhaps part of the right-hand stroke may be detected. Other possibilities for the quota of 300 drachmai (as also in line 26) are *'Ερετριε̃ς*,

[11] McGregor, in 1934, preferred *οι̣* to *ον̣*; *A.T.L.*, I, p. 96; see also Meritt, *Athenian Financial Documents* (1932), p. 10, who leaned to *ον̣*. Mattingly, *Historia*, X (1961), pp. 167–68 with notes 88 and 89, thought *ον̣* "at least as likely" as *οι̣* and used the former in his restoration. He has now changed his mind again and takes *οι̣* to be the final letters of the last Thracian ethnic in the panel above; *B.S.A.*, LXV (1970), pp. 139–40. Our iota is apparently centered, without any other trace, and it is the last letter of the line; consequently our preference approaches conviction.

[12] It is this kind of error that makes us so sceptical of the reporting of Rangabé and Pittakys.

[13] *Urkunden und Untersuchungen zur Geschichte des delisch-attischen Bundes* (1870), Plate IX, no. 105*a*.

Κεῖοι, Σίφνιοι, all of which appear in List 25, and *Κύθνιοι* (List 22 and A9) and *'Εφαιστιε̂ς* (List 22, with an uncertain quota, and A9).

Line 23: We see enough of the letters printed to make the reading sure: the horizontals of epsilon, the bow of rho, the upper tips of the iotas, the circular scar of omicron. We cannot identify any trace of the first letter.

Line 24: Of alpha we claim only the crossbar. The vertical and the middle horizontal of epsilon and the bottom of the left stroke of nu are present. The mason crowded the letters of this entry, as is evident from what is extant of epsilon and nu. If the restoration is correct, the average width of the *stoichos* in the line is 0.0135 m., whereas the standard in this area is 0.015 m. In lines 23 and 24 Pittakys[14] read *Περίνθιοι* and *Βεργαῖοι*, strange intruders in the Nesiotic panel! See note 12 above.

Lines 26–28: In a number of lists (see Lists 12, 13, 14, 15, 20, 22) *'Εφαιστιε̂ς, Μυριναῖοι*, and *"Ιμβριοι* are entered as a group near the end or at the end (14, 15, 20, 22) of the Nesiotic panel. It is tempting to restore here:

HHH	[*'Εφαιστιε̂ς*]
------	[*Μυριναῖοι*]
------	[*"Ιμβριοι*]

We should then have partial payments for Myrina and Imbros with the complements acknowledged in I, 18–19.

Line 31: We remove the question-mark from the quota and understand that Kyzikos made a total payment of 9 talents (see I, 10 for the complement), as in the previous period. The two payments in List 25 left Kyzikos a few drachmai short of fulfilling its obligation in 430/29.

Line 35: The record of Lampsakos is erratic but its pre-war assessment appears to have been 12 talents. The two quotas of List 25 (1,045 + 146+ dr.) show that the assessed total was

[14] *'Εφ. 'Αρχ.*, 1853, no. 1252.

not quite reached. We restore the quota of Lampsakos in 26, I, 4 as [XΔ]ΔΔΓ and relate it to the newly established quota of III, 35 to produce a total of 1,171 dr. This is so like the record of Lampsakos in the previous year that we do not hesitate to restore the ethnic in this line. This is not the only case in which the majority of the payment is booked in the appendix; see I, 8–9 for Madytos and Elaious.

Line 37: What we interpret as a drachma and an obol looks rather like the squared top of a pi, with both angles preserved. The omicron is a series of punches forming the expected rounding. Despite obvious crowding, the lower tip of a vertical in the next *stoichos* is too close to omicron to be read comfortably as iota. Our restoration is not beyond doubt.

Line 38: We perceive most of alpha in the third *stoichos*. The top of omicron in the fifth *stoichos* survives in color; the bottom and right side are cutting; on the left a series of punches joins color and cutting. The possible restorations are [*Κι*]α[ν]ο[ί] and [*Νε*]ά[π]ο[λις].

Line 39: The vertical in the column of numerals, part color and part cutting, falls below the right vertical of Γ in line 35. Color and cutting identify the vertical of epsilon and its lowest horizontal; the top horizontal is cutting, the middle color. The traces of the horizontals do not extend to the vertical. Only the bottom part of iota can be seen, centrally cut.

Line 41: Most of upsilon, partly in color, is identifiable. Candidates for restoration are [*Ἀβ*]υ[δενοί] and [*Δα*]υ[νιοτειχῖται].

Line 49: We note a left-hand diagonal and a short base; whether these are the marks of the chisel or accidental scratches we are not sure. Similarly, a central vertical and a horizontal extending to the right, which we print as a doubtful tau, may not in fact be the mason's cutting.

Lines 51–53: We repeat the readings of Rangabé[15] because they preserve a substantial portion of credible names and it is not easy to imagine how he could have invented them. We

15 *Ant. Hell.*, I, no. 224.

ourselves can claim no more than a doubtful pi, the initial letter of line 51; the strokes seem more like scratches than cutting and the horizontal slopes downward from left to right. What might be taken for alpha (lacking the right side) is in fact between the second and third *stoichoi* and can scarcely be a letter. We restore the quota of Parion to complete a full payment along with the complement in I, 7. In List 25 (III, 24 and 50) the city failed by a few drachmai to complete its obligation.

Lines 54–55: Rangabé's reading (*loc. cit.*) was adopted in *A.T.L.*, II, and restored as *'Ελαι*[*όσιοι*] | *ἐν* [*X*]*ε*[*ρρονέσοι*]. This we discard, albeit with reluctance, since only this entry fits what we read in lines 56–57. It is true that the epsilon (the three horizontals are legible) of line 55 is, if anything, slightly left of the fourth *stoichos*. We assume pronounced crowding to accommodate the long ethnic that we restore.

Lines 56–57: If the *stoichos* is 0.015 m. in width, then omicron is the eighth letter. So in the next line omicrons may be read in the seventh and eleventh *stoichoi*. Of the final iota, only the upper part is cutting; there is color at the foot. The first omicron of this line is quite convincing. Only [*ἐν Χερρ*]*ο*[*νέσ*]*οι* fits our reading of line 57; hence our restoration of the two lines as a single entry.

Line 58: The top of iota shows color; the letter, cut between the eleventh and twelfth *stoichoi*, reflects the crowding that one could expect in a long ethnic. Only the upper left-hand arc of omicron can be detected, chiefly by the color. In lines 57 and 58 [*Μαδύτι*]*οι* and [*Λιμναῖ*]*οι* are restored in *A.T.L.*, II. The readings appear first in Meritt's text of 1927,[16] where no indication of their position in the lines is given. We read final OI in line 57 but the ending belongs to a long name. The restorations of *A.T.L.*, II, must be rejected.

Line 59: In the fourth space of the column of numerals we read a doubtful vertical. The following delta is more con-

[16] *A.J.A.*, XXXI (1927), p. 183.

vincing. We restore the quota as for Byzantion, in conjunction with the complement recorded in I, 5, to give a total of 2,911 + drachmai. This accords with the record of List 25, where the two payments fall a little short of 3,000 drachmai. We conjecture that the assessment was 30 talents. It is not impossible that the quota of this line should be attributed to Abydos (see I, 6, where the complement cannot be restored). We are not absolutely certain that line 59 was the last entry of the column.

COLUMN IV

Again, we restrict our commentary to changes of substance. Throughout this column there is considerable variation in the lateral spacing of letters. This may be observed at the top, where the ends of lines 9, 10, 13, 14, 15, and 21 can be read with assurance.

Line 15: The assessment of Halikarnassos had been 1 talent 4,000 drachmai in the previous period and indeed had varied only in the second period. We therefore restore the normal quota here.

Line 16: We read part of the lower right-hand arc of omicron and most of iota. The candidates for restoration are [*Κολοφόνι*]*οι* and [*Τελάνδρι*]*οι*. Kolophon had been taken by the Persians in the early summer of 430 B.C. (Thucydides, III, 34, 1); later the loyal Kolophonians were settled in Notion (Thucydides, III, 34, 4). They paid a token tribute in the spring of 427 B.C. (List 27, III, 24). It is a question whether they were in a position to pay anything in 429/8 and perhaps [*Τελάνδρι*]*οι* is to be preferred in this line.

Line 19: Iota is sure. Alpha is a combination of color and cutting.

Line 21: We restore the normal quota of Elaiea.

Line 22: The top and bottom strokes of sigma are present. The possibilities are [*Ἀστυπαλαιε͂*]*ς* and [*Διάκριοι ἐχ*]*ς* [*Ῥόδο*].

Line 36: We see all the epsilon except the top horizontal.

Line 37: In some lights the tau is unmistakable. If the epsilon of line 36 is in the twelfth *stoichos*, this tau is in the thirteenth, which fits no Karian name. We therefore suppose that the letters of *Μύνδιοι παρὰ Τέρμ* were widely spaced and that the place-name was abbreviated by suspension: *Τέρμ*(*ερα*).

Line 38: We report the left side of omicron with doubt, the lower half of sigma with confidence (slightly left of the sigma of [*h*]*αιρ*[*αι*]*ε̂ς* in line 44). We base the restoration on omicron in the second *stoichos*.

Line 39: If we take [*Β*]*ọ*[*υθειε̂*]*ς* as a model, our firmly read epsilon is the eleventh letter. But epsilon and sigma (the whole lower half is legible) are widely spaced.

Line 40: We interpret the vertical (with a mild slope) in the fourth *stoichos* as kappa; there is a suggestion of arms. The first alpha depends on the left-hand diagonal (which, to be sure, seems a little high), the tau on the complete upper half; only the upper half of the right-hand diagonal is missing from alpha and the bottom third from iota. [*Χαλ*]*κ̣*[*ει*]*α̣̂ται* is the obvious restoration. Again, the spacing is not quite regular (although the first alpha lies almost over the epsilon of [*hα*]*ιρ*[*α*]*ιε̂*[*ς*] in line 45; but see the note *ad loc.*). The apparent lower and right side of a circular letter between the first and second *stoichoi* cannot be authentic cutting.

Line 42: Epsilon lacks only the middle horizontal; it is probably the sixth letter, since it falls directly over the second iota of line 45 ([*hα*]*ιρ*[*α*]*ιε̂*[*ς*]). Possible restorations are [*Καμιρ*]*ε̂*[*ς*], [*Κεδρι*]*ε̂*[*ται*], [*Ναχσι*]*ε̂*[*ται*], and [*Πυγελ*]*ε̂*[*ς*]. The letter before epsilon may be rho.

Lines 44–45: Our readings confirm the restorations of *A.T.L.*, II. Notice the irregularity of the spacing; curiously, the letters of the ethnic in line 45 (which adds *περυσι*[*ν*]*ô*) fall slightly to the right of the same letters in line 44. In this case the mason's vagaries are manifest.

Lines 48–49: The tau in line 49 is firm; we are less sure of the vertical read as iota. The latter is placed under the first iota of

[*Μαρ*]*αθέσιοι* and so we make it the eighth letter. Between it and tau there is space for two letters. There is no other possible restoration.

Line 50: The letters survive in their entirety. Possible restorations are [*Καλύδνι*]*οι*, [*Καρπάθι*]*οι*, and [*Πιταναῖ*]*οι*.

Line 52: The top half of sigma is visible immediately below the omicron of line 50; two letter-spaces intervene between this and a complete iota.

Lines 57–58: The restorations [*Π*]*ριαν*[*ε̂ς*] and [*Κ*]*ο̂*[*ι*]*ο*[*ι*] in *A.T.L.*, II, depend upon the readings of Rangabé (*loc. cit.*). These we reject. The first letter of line 57 appears to be circular; it may have inspired Rangabé's rho. We venture two verticals, one in the seventh *stoichos* (below sigma of [*Μαρ*]*αθέσιοι*), one in the twelfth (one beyond the final iota of [*Χερρονέ*]*σ*[*ιο*]*ι* in line 52); the latter we interpret as kappa in order to find a restoration that accords with the physical remains. We see no credible evidence of engraving in line 58. The only possible circular scar lies to the left of the first *stoichos*. Line 57 may have been the last of the column.

COLUMN I

We have carefully measured the left lateral side in order to compute the number of numerals lost with fragment 2, which was seen only by Pittakys,[17] whose publication we employ with caution in restoration. In general we agree with the text of *A.T.L.*, II. Elsewhere we comment.

Line 3: Our reading is [. . .]ΔͰ. A corner of delta remains; the whole was seen by Pittakys. The first payment of Dardanos is no longer extant in column III; this complement should have brought the total quota to 100 drachmai (cf. 25, III, 31 and 52). We cannot tell whether the first figure was 𐅄 or Δ.

Line 4: See the commentary on III, 35. The extant reading is [. . .]ΔΓ. Pittakys saw two deltas.

[17] *L'ancienne Athènes* (1835), pp. 411–12.

Line 5: We read [. . .]ℲIII. Pittakys gives IΓHHII. His second H is an error for Ⲏ, as may be seen today, even on the photograph (*A.T.L.*, I, p. 95). In *A.T.L.*, I, it was assumed that his ΓH, as so often, represented ᴾ. We have preferred to interpret this as ᴾH and to force his initial half-vertical into a chi; see the commentary on III, 59.

Line 6: The spacing is ours, the obols come from Pittakys. The payment of Abydos is not preserved in column III.

Line 7: We read [. . .]ⱵⱵ; Pittakys IH. For the restoration see the commentary on III, 51.

Line 8: We read [. . .]ⱵⱵ; Pittakys Δ.

Line 9: We read [. . .]ⱵⱵ; Pittakys ΔΔII.

Line 10: We read [.]ΔΔⱵⱵ; Pittakys ΔΔ.

Line 13: The first payment, now lost, was recorded in column III.

Lines 18–19: See the commentary on III, 26–28.

THE DATE

We have no intention of entering upon a long discussion of the date of List 26, which, after a detailed re-examination of the evidence, we regard as secure, 429/8 B.C., as in *A.T.L.*, I and II. Nevertheless, since this dating has been attacked by Mattingly, we cite what we regard as the determining arguments.[18] We first set out in tabular form our views and those of Mattingly

[18] Mattingly, *Historia*, X (1961), pp. 166–68; *Class. Quart.*, N.S. XI (1961), pp. 155–60; XVI (1966), pp. 179–83; *B.S.A.*, LXV (1970), pp. 133–42. F. A. Lepper expressed qualms; *J.H.S.*, LXXXII (1962), pp. 27–28. Mattingly was answered cogently, we think, by B. D. Meritt and H. T. Wade-Gery, *J.H.S.*, LXXXII (1962), pp. 73–74, and by Meritt, *G.R.B.S.*, VIII (1967), pp. 50–52. The case for the present dating was first made at length by Meritt, *A.F.D.*, pp. 3–25; see *D.A.T.*, pp. 98–100. The argument is summarized and supplemented in *A.T.L.*, I, pp. 191–99 (commentary on Lists 25–27), and III, pp. 69–70. Mattingly's latest effort is to us no more convincing than his earlier treatments and does not demand detailed refutation. It is an apt comment on his method that, tucked away at the end of note 35 (*B.S.A.*, LXV [1970], p. 135), is a renunciation of his assignment of the foundation of Brea to 426/5; this date had been the keystone of his previous discussion of the problem.

concerning assessments and lists from 430/29 to 425/4; we use the notation of *A.T.L.*

	A.T.L.	*Mattingly*
430/29	Assessment (A7); List 25	Assessment (A7).
429/8	List 26	List 28
428/7	Assessment (A8); List 27	List 27
427/6	List 28 (which may be 29)	List 26
426/5	[List 29] (see above)	Assessment (A8); List 25
425/4	Assessment (A9)	Assessment (A9)

1. The striking correspondences, especially in the nature of the Hellespontine payments, and the constancy of the quotas prove that Lists 25 and 26 belong not only in consecutive years but also in the same assessment period.

2. List 27, because of its scale of quotas, must come before the impressive increases of A9. It differs from Lists 25 and 26 in several respects: (a) *Ἀναφαῖοι, Σεριοτειχῖται, Σομβία, Ἄμιοι, Λερ[. . . .]ι* appear for the first time; (b) *Κάσιοι, Βέσβικος*, and *Ἐτεοκαρπάθιοι*, previously entered under special rubrics, graduate to regular panels; (c) *Κλαζομένιοι, Πολιχνῖται*, and *Ἐρυθραῖοι* suffer increases of tribute;[19] (d) Nisyros is Ionic in List 27, Insular in 26 (III, 20). List 27, therefore, cannot be assigned to the same period as 25–26; moreover, it must belong later. There had been, therefore, an assessment between 430 and 425 (A9). Thucydides notes four tribute-collecting expeditions: winter 430/29 (II, 69), winter 428/7 (III, 19), winter 425/4 (IV, 50, 1), early summer 424 (IV, 75). He specifically mentions the Athenians' need of money in 428/7 (III, 19, 1). We associate these expeditions with assessments: we have A9 (425/4) and 430/29 (A7) was a regular Panathenaic year, so A8 may logically be restored to 428. List 27 reflects that assessment.[20]

[19] *Κνίδιοι* pay less (2 talents); they last appear in 440/39, paying 3 talents.

[20] Meritt, *A.F.D.*, pp. 17–18, and *A.T.L.*, I, p. 198, and III, p. 70, urge that the absence of the Aktaian cities means that List 27 must be dated earlier than 427/6, *i.e.*, 428/7. The argument, we think, is not conclusive; we cannot know how the Athenians dealt with the new tributaries before 425/4, when they occupied a separate panel in the assessment. But List 28 is of the same period as List 27 (*A.T.L.*, I, p. 199); thus we have two lists for the three-year period, in which there is no room for Lists 25 and 26.

In consequence, Lists 25 and 26 may continue to reside in Period 7 (430/29–429/8).

3. We call attention to the records of Hairai and Pygela:

23, I, 37	H	*hαιραῖοι*
List 24	Lost	
25, I, 43	------	[*hαιραι*]ε̂ς *hένο*[21]
26, IV, 44–45	[H]	[*h*]αιρ[αι]ε̂ς
	[H]	[*hα*]ιρ[α]ιε̂[ς] περυσι[ν]ô
25, I, 45–46	-------	[*Πυγελ*]ε̂ς
	-------	[*Πυγε*]λε̂ς *hένες* ἐπιφορᾶς

The most reasonable explanation of Hairai's eccentricities is that the state paid in full in 432/1 (List 23), defaulted in 431/0 (List 24), paid its arrears but not its current debt in 430/29 (List 25), paid its arrears as well as its current instalment in 429/8 (List 26). This reconstruction dates the lists; in any case, our reading of the prescript (above, pp. 10–11) forces List 26 into 429/8, now that later years are barred. Mattingly attacks the restoration of [*hαιραι*]ε̂ς in List 25: "[*Γρυνει*]ε̂ς is there a perfectly acceptable substitute."[22] Possibly so; but Mattingly overlooks the common association of *Λεβέδιοι* and *hαιραιε̂ς* (lines 42–43) in the lists (9, [12], 13, 15, 16), which supports the restoration [*hαιραι*]ε̂ς.[23]

To judge from our extant lists, the infliction of *ἐπιφορά* ceased at the end of Period 6 (431/0); that is, it was not to be collected in the next period. In List 25 Pygela is credited with *ἐπιφορά* for the previous year, which did not transgress the new policy. Again, List 25 must therefore be the first record of a period, that is, it is appropriately placed in 430/29.

The order of districts, of which Mattingly makes a great deal, does not seem to us a weighty matter. It is true that generally the order remained the same in the lists of a given period; it is

[21] The quota should probably be restored as [H].

[22] *Class Quart.*, N.S. XI (1961), p. 155.

[23] See the geographical argument for the restoration of lines 41–46 in *A.T.L.*, I, p. 192.

true that the order in Lists 25 and 26 differs. This seems trivial against the other evidence that we have cited.[24]

Our intention was not to argue at length the question of date but, rather, to seek evidence in scrupulous examination of the prescript and the columns. This we have done. In a sense, the prescript did not fulfill our hopes, although we obtained, we think, physical evidence for the length of line, about which we had entertained doubts. This reinforced our conviction that List 26 is properly dated in 429/8.

[24] To recapitulate: 25 and 26 (in that order) *must* belong to consecutive years of the same period and *must* precede 27 (and probably 28), which *must* be assigned to a different period, before A9. Why is the order of districts used by Thoudippos in his decree (A9) different from the order of the assessment proper? We do not answer this question but we are sure that it is not because he took the trouble to consult and imitate the order of the quota-list of the previous year. There was no "official" order; a secretary, preparing his accounts, might well copy from his predecessors.

CHAPTER II

Regulations for Miletos

[Plates IV–VII]

A re-examination in Athens of *I.G.*, I², 22+, the Regulations for Miletos,[1] has produced a revised text that will appear in the projected third edition of *Inscriptiones Graecae*, I. We present here an explanation and commentary in justification of this text and of a new reconstruction of the stele. Although it is a commonplace that the inscription is too fragmentary for any precise determination of all its provisions,[2] it nonetheless seems worth-while to make public a detailed commentary on what we think can be extracted from it. This, we hope, will dispel some misconceptions and perhaps cast some light on the problem of its date, which has been much debated recently.[3]

[1] The basic edition is by J. H. Oliver, "The Athenian Decree Concerning Miletus in 450/49 B.C.," *T.A.P.A.*, LXVI (1935), pp. 177–98 with Plates 1 (photograph) and 2 (drawing) = *S.E.G.*, X, 14 (henceforth Oliver), who added a fragment. We know of only two texts published since that time, neither of them based on autopsy: A. G. Woodhead, D11 in *A.T.L.*, II, pp. 58–60 (henceforth Woodhead), and H. Bengtson, *Die Staatsverträge des Altertums*, II, no. 151, pp. 60–64 (henceforth Bengtson). We refer to the fragments by Oliver's designation (see his Plate 1 opposite p. 198): frag. *a* = EM 6802, frag. *b* = EM 6801, frags. *c* and *d* = EM 5330, frag. *e* = EM 6801α, frags. *f*, *g*, *h* = EM 5329. These fragments will be labeled from 1 to 8 in the new edition of *Inscriptiones Graecae*, I.

[2] See Woodhead, p. 60.

[3] The orthodox dating (450/49 B.C.) has been attacked by H. B. Mattingly, *Historia*, X (1961), pp. 174–81; *Class. Quart.*, N.S. XVI (1966), pp. 189–90; *Ancient Society and Institutions*, ed. E. Badian (henceforth *A.S. & I.*), pp. 207–209; *Acta of the Fifth International Congress of Greek and Latin Epigraphy Cambridge 1967*,

Eight fragments of the monument survive, of which the bottom six join one another. We noted, however, that in the stele as reconstructed in the Epigraphical Museum the two non-joining fragments at the top, *a* and *b*, were not in the position that Oliver had suggested. Both were too high and *b* lay much too far to the right.[4] With the permission and encouragement of Mrs. Dina Peppas-Delmouzou, Director of the Museum, we had these pieces removed from the plaster. It became immediately apparent that Oliver's placement of *a* and *b* in relationship to one another was correct, since the lines of vertical break on the left of *b* and the right of *a* matched perfectly (see Plate IV). We then followed Oliver's method by placing these two pieces in such a position that *a* was the correct distance from the left edge, as determined by the formula in line 2, and the lines of cleavage at both the fronts and backs of *b* and *c* were aligned. The results were close to

---

pp. 31–32. It has been defended by J. P. Barron, *J.H.S.*, LXXXII (1962), pp. 1–6; B. D. Meritt and H. T. Wade-Gery, *J.H.S.*, LXXXIII (1963), pp. 100–102; R. Meiggs, *H.S.C.P.*, LXVII (1963), pp. 24–25; *J.H.S.*, LXXXVI (1966), p. 95. P. Herrmann, "Zu den Beziehungen zwischen Athen und Milet im 5. Jahrhundert," *Klio*, LII (1970), pp. 163–73, leaves open the date of this inscription and concludes that the new Milesian decree edited by him does not solve the problem. It is clear to us, however, that the early date 437/6 best fits the new document, which has a preamble implying an Athenian-style democracy at Miletos. This supports the orthodox dating of *I.G.*, I^2, 22.

[4] The misplacement of *b* to the right may have been caused by its position in the photographs in Oliver, Plate 1, and *A.T.L.*, II, Plate IV, especially the latter. The error in height probably arose from a misinterpretation of Oliver's proposal (p. 183) "that the cleavage visible on fragment *b* is a continuation of the cleavage visible on the upper part of fragment *c*." The fractures suffered by *b* and *c* are similar in that in each case the break at the surface continues diagonally towards the upper left until it reaches the back of the stone; thus a rough and receding shelf is created, as is best realized by an examination of Plates IV and V. Oliver's "cleavage" must refer to the break at the back, *i.e.*, at the extreme upper left of the stones, where the break reaches the back. In the Museum's reconstruction, on the other hand, the line of break at the surface on the bottom (*i.e.*, right side) of *b* running from upper right to lower left was aligned with the break at the surface at the top (left) of *c*; the photograph published in the paper-back edition of Woodhead's *The Study of Greek Inscriptions* (opposite p. 64) is, probably, of the restored stele but has been manipulated to bring *b* to the left and down and thus into a more correct relationship with *a* and *c*.

Plate IV. *I.G.*, I^{2}, 22 (D11), Regulations for Miletos, showing the relationship between the upper fragments (*a* left, *b* right) (*Photograph by D. R. Laing*)

Plate V. *I.G.*, I^2, 22 (D11), fragments *a*, *b*, and *c* (the lower fragment), illustrating the "shelf" created by the fractures of *b* and *c* (*Photograph by D. R. Laing*)

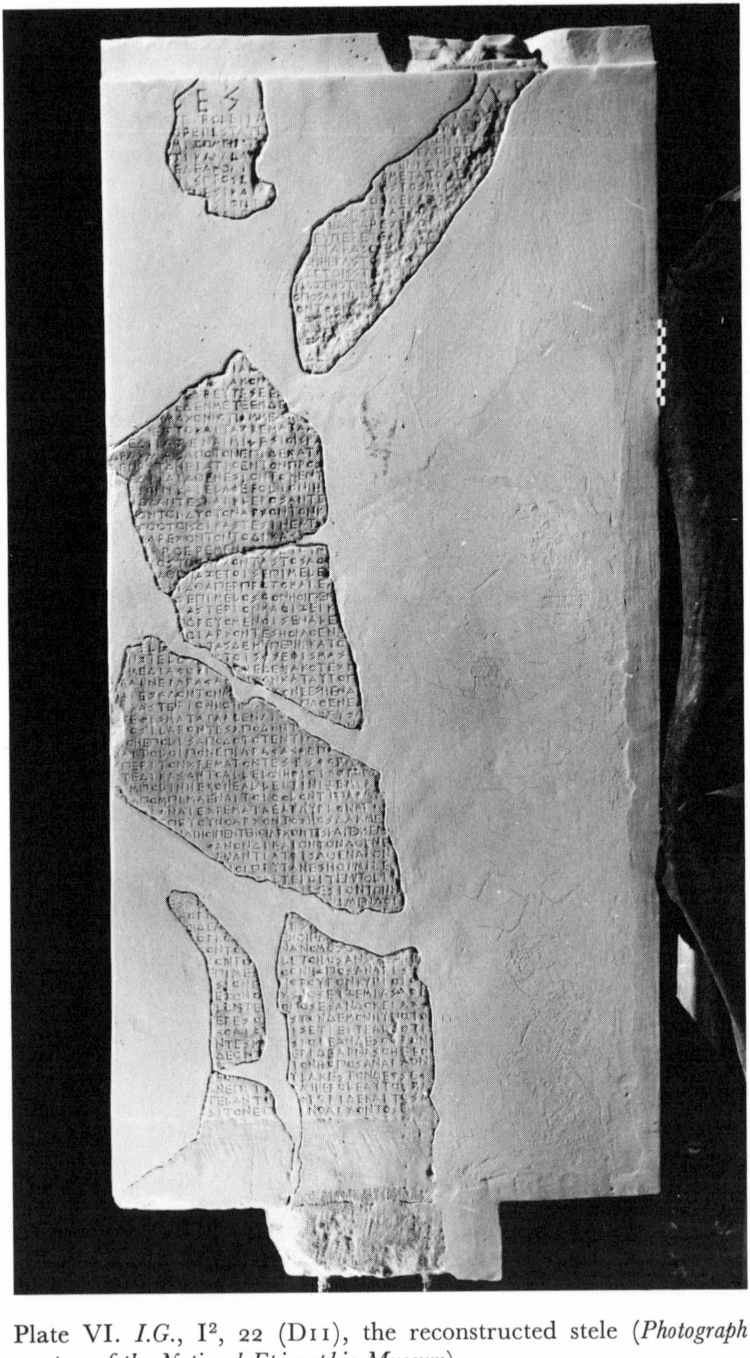

Plate VI. *I.G.*, I², 22 (D11), the reconstructed stele (*Photograph courtesy of the National Epigraphic Museum*)

Plate VII. *I.G.*, I², 22 (D11), fragment *a* (*Photograph by D. R. Laing*)

Oliver's; the upper fragments rested only slightly lower, so that the bottom two lines of *b* overlapped the top two of *c*.[5] The line of vertical break on *b* was thus slightly to the left of that on *c*, which conforms to the direction of the fracture from the bottom to the top of the stele. The precise position of *a* in relation to the left edge was further controlled by the use of a ruler on the margin and by alignment of the *stoichoi* with those of *c;* there was no discrepancy. We used the latter method because we had become convinced that the stone had very little taper and that the number of *stoichoi* remained constant at 58 throughout the entire length, not increasing to 62 or 64, as previously thought. It is to this question that we now turn.

It has been recognized since the time of St. A. Koumanoudes that this text was cut *stoichedon* with some irregularities.[6] Oliver (p. 184) saw that these were frequently caused by the crowding of an iota or the *daseia*, but he also believed that some displacements were the result of the addition of letters that increased the length of line; he seems to have missed the fact that at times one letter occupied two spaces and that this phenomenon created the illusion in the following line that the length was gradually increasing.[7] Woodhead (p. 60) noted all but one of the cases of one letter occupying two spaces, but he continued to accept the proposition that the length of line increased. Although he realized that the displacements in lines

[5] See Plate V. Cf. the photograph in Oliver, where *b* is in a position that denies overlapping and is also too far to the right of *a*. It is obvious that, if *b* were moved to the left to suit its relationship with *a*, it would in addition have to be lowered to make the lines of cleavage match.

[6] *Ἀθήναιον*, V (1876), pp. 82–85 (frags. *b*, *c*, *d*, *g*, *h*), 167 (frag. *a*); VI (1877), pp. 127–28 (frags. *f* and *h*).

[7] *E.g.*, Oliver writes (p. 184) of lines 57–59 (by his numbering 59–61): "Another unobtrusive insertion occurs in line 59, where the letters *ONHOI* occupy the space of three letters above. It is one of the common cases of crowding in the presence of an aspirate or of an iota. In line 60, however, one letter falls below the *ON* and another below each of the other three crowded letters. Lines 61 ff. continue the new arrangement of line 60, and the normal line has again become longer by one letter space." But it is an epsilon occupying two spaces in line 56 that creates the whole illusion. Woodhead (p. 60) observed that the plan of line 58 is the same as that of line 55.

57–59 did not indicate increase, he believed that those in lines 27–31 did. There too, however, it is only the epsilon in line 28 and the mu in line 30, each occupying two *stoichoi*, that give the illusion of increase. His contention that the eleventh letter of line 2 (beta) lies vertically over the twelfth of line 31 (tau) and the tenth of 32 (theta) over the eleventh of 55 (nu) must have been based upon his assignment of too much taper to the stele. This seems to be why he sees the vertical *stoichoi* as "edging away to the left," which, incidentally, is hardly consonant with his introduction of a new letter-space at the beginning of line 27. If the stele is reconstructed with less taper, in obedience to the extant evidence, the *stoichoi* fall into place regularly below one another and the length of the line remains therefore uniform.

In analyzing the irregularities in the pattern we were struck by the realization that almost all could be explained by the following hypothesis. The mason,[8] using some perishable material such as chalk, laid out in an almost perfect *stoichedon* pattern a text that contained a number of Ionicisms. But before the actual cutting was begun an official of some sort ordered these changed to Attic and other errors corrected. Instead of redesigning the whole inscription, the stone-cutter merely emended: he erased as necessary and he rewrote, thus marring the *stoichedon* arrangement. Of the thirty-three instances of irregularity detectable on the stone, this hypothesis explains all but four. The latter are cases in which iota is crowded in after omicron, with no involvement of the *daseia*. Three are the ending of the dative plural;[9] the other occurs in the restored participle οἰ[κôντες].[10] These we take to be an idiosyncrasy of the mason, for they are too numerous to be mere errors, even

[8] It seems almost certain that the engraving was carried out by at least two masons, since after about line 32 there are striking changes in the forms of zeta, nu, pi, and upsilon. We assume, but of course cannot be sure, that these were idiosyncracies of the cutting, not of the original layout.

[9] Lines 15, 29, 36; see also the almost certain restoration in line 6.

[10] Line 57; see the commentary *ad loc.*

though the letters *OI* of the dative plural are symmetrically inscribed seven times.[11]

Of the twenty-nine remaining irregularities, nineteen can be accounted for by the assumption that aspirates were added to the original text. Where this was done, three letters occupy two spaces twelve times;[12] two occupy one four times;[13] four occupy three twice and five occupy four once.[14] In contrast, there are thirteen cases on the stone where the aspirate had obviously owned its *stoichos* from the beginning;[15] in two places it should have been added but was not.[16] In four other cases there is no sign of crowding where an aspirate would be expected just to the left of the break in the stone.[17] It is remarkable that the first sure example of the *daseia* cut alone in its *stoichos* does not occur until line 46; the second is in line 58 and from here on sole occupancy is more common than crowding, eleven cases to four. This supports the conjecture that the original text contained no aspirates and that, before completion of the original draft on the stone, the mason was instructed to insert them in Attic style but did so carelessly. Of this conjecture we cannot, of course, be sure, but it is likely enough to make suspect the restoration of an aspirate alone in its *stoichos* in the first part of the text.[18]

In the remaining ten examples of irregularities in the *stoichedon* arrangement there is further evidence of Ionicisms in the text first submitted to the mason. One is particularly

[11] Lines 7, 38, 40, 44, 47, 64, 79.

[12] Lines 14, 16, 19, 22, 27, 33, 42, 45, 46, 57, 70, 71. The initial vertical in line 81 *may* be the iota of [*ho*]*ί*, or it may be part of nu; we do not count it in our statistics.

[13] Lines 51, 53, 66, 84.

[14] Lines 50 and 54; and 17. In lines 3 and 4 the restoration of crowded aspirates seems necessary; these we do not count, however.

[15] Lines 46, 58, 61, 65 (twice), 67, 73 (twice), 74, 77, 78, 81, 82; the upper right vertical in line 23 has been read as *H* but we doubt this interpretation.

[16] Lines 5, 12.

[17] Lines 11, 45, 68, 83; there may be another case in line 71 (see the note *ad loc.*).

[18] See the commentary on lines 4, 11, 23.

instructive: in line 3 the nu is crowded into the word [χ]συνγγρα[φε̂ς]. This strange spelling is best explained by the assumption that the stone-cutter, told to spell the word in Attic style, with nu, added the letter without removing the gamma that it should have replaced. In the six cases in which letters are spread, three are obviously caused by the substitution of Attic *E* for Ionic *EI*: ε̂ναι (line 29), προερεμένο[ι]ς (line 38), and ἐσφορᾶ[ς] (line 56). A fourth, ἔστο (line 28), may be an amendment of the unexampled form εἴστο, although it is more probable that we have here a blunder by the scribe or mason, who perhaps unthinkingly had εἰς τό in his mind. A fifth case has Attic *O* for Ionic *OY*, τό[ς] (line 9).[19] The final case, δραχμάς in line 30, must be explained as a stone-cutter's error; mu is in any event a wide letter. Faulty engraving is probably responsible for the two curious *vacats* in lines 63 and 64. The only other irregularity is the crowding in line 62 where thirty letters are compressed into twenty-two spaces and it is impossible to know how much more crowding there was to the right and left of the preserved stone. This must have been caused by a major error in the first draft on the stele or a considerable change of text.

Thus, we believe, the irregularities in the *stoichedon* pattern can be understood. There is one other non-Attic spelling in the text: συν- in line 6, where we expect χσυν-. This, however, is the only extant example of this word in this text, whether as preposition or as prefix. Sigma may, therefore, have been the standard spelling throughout, although the restoration of line 3 almost demands χσ-.

The text, then, should be reconstructed with fifty-eight *stoichoi* to the line throughout. These average 0.0143 m. vertically; horizontally they measure *ca* 0.0114 m. near the

[19] Ionic texts vary between τός and τούς. For τούς see the Aphytaian fragment of the Decree of Klearchos on coinage, *A.T.L.*, II, D14, frag. 3, line 21 (p. 64); τός occurs in frag. 5 (from Siphnos), line 5 (p. 65).

top of the stone and 0.0116 m. near the bottom. The stone had very little taper, increasing in width from *ca* 0.668 m. at line 10 to *ca* 0.678 m. at line 82. The height of the stele, including the fragmentary sculpture at the top and the tenon at the bottom, is 1.517 m.; the inscribed face measures 1.363 m.

Our text itself is very conservative and includes only those restorations that we feel are certain. Yet we think it worthwhile to discuss in the commentary the supplements offered by previous editors that are not made impossible by the correct positioning of the fragments. Many of these, particularly those of Oliver (who did not claim literal accuracy; see his p. 177), deserve more respect than they have been accorded. We believe that only from the intimacy that is acquired by persistent attempts to restore will a clear idea of the sense of much of the original text emerge. A mere perusal of the surviving text will not suffice, for isolated words can easily give a false impression (see, *e.g.*, ἐ̲σφορᾶ[ς] in line 56 and the commentary *ad loc.*).

In the text that we proffer here, the brace indicates that one less *stoichos* is occupied than the letters enclosed, the underlining that an additional *stoichos* has been used; line 62, which we have underlined, is an exception, for here thirty letters are forced into twenty-two *stoichoi*.

Our own examination has led to a number of adjustments in the readings. Where these are minor, we make no specific mention of them; where they cause major changes we add the label BM to the lemma. McGregor inherited A. B. West's copy of *Inscriptiones Graecae*, I^2, in which the present document (*I.G.*, I^2, 22) is heavily annotated. These notes have proved valuable to us and where appropriate we have attributed to *West* restorations derived from them; in some cases West anticipated our own proposals. The label West refers to restorations acknowledged as his by Oliver.

450/49 B.C. ΣΤΟΙΧ. 58

[Μι]λεσί̣[οις χσυγ]γρ[αφαί]
[ἔδοχσεν] τε͂ι βολε͂ι κα[ὶ τõι δέμοι, . . . 6 . . ι̇ς ἐπρ]υτάν[ευε, . ±6 . . . ἐγραμμάτ]
[ευε, . ±4 .]ορ ἐπεστάτε, [Εὔθυνος ἐ͂ρχε· τάδε hοι χ]συγγρα[φε͂ς χσυνέγραφσαν· τε]
[λε͂ν τὰ ν]ομιζόμενα το[ῖς θεοῖς, hαιρε͂σθαι δ]ὲ πέντε ἄν[δρας τὸν δε͂μον ἐχς hαπ]
[άντον α]ὐτίκα μάλα ὐ̣[πὲρ πεντέκοντα ἔτε] γεγονότ[ας, ἐχσομοσίαν δὲ μὲ ἐ͂να]
[ι αὐτοῖς μ]εδὲ ἀνθ⟨α⟩ί[ρεσιν, τούτος δὲ ἄρ]χεν καὶ συν[. . . . . 19 . . . .]
[. . . 7 . . .]οις προσερ̣[. . . . . 13 . . . . .]ι μετὰ το α̣ι̣[. . . . . 20 . . . .]
[. . . 8 . . . .]ενεσι καὶ τ̣ο[. . . 10 . . . .]γος τὸς Μιλ[εσίον . . . . . . 16 . . . . . .]
[. . . 7 . . . Μιλ]εσίον τὸ[ς . . . 7 . . .]ο̣γος ΔΕΚΑΤΟ[. . . . . 22 . . . .]
[. . . . 11 . . . .] τριερ̣[. . . 8 . . . .] τ̣õν στρατιο[τ]ί̣δ[ον . . . . 19 . . . .]
[. . . . . 22 . . . .] ὅπλα παρέχεσθαι κ̣[. . . . . 21 . . . .]
[. . . . . 22 . . . .]ε· ὐπερετε͂ν [δ]ὲ τού[τοις . . . . 18 . . . .]
[. . . . . 20 . . . . τέ]τταρας ὀβο[λὸ]ς π[. . . . . 23 . . . .]
[. . . . . 21 . . . .]ον hεκ⟨ά⟩στο [τõ] σόμ̣[ατος . . . . 20 . . . .]
[. . . . . . 16 . . . . . . Ἀθέν]α̣ζε τοῖς στρ[α]τιό[τεσι . . . . 21 . . . .]
[. . . . . . . 17 . . . . . . Ἀθέ]ναζε hότι δ' ἄ̣[ν] τὸ [. . . . . 26 . . . .]
[. . . . . 19 . . . . h]οπόσα ἂν λάβο[σι . . . . 26 . . . .]
[. . . . . 20 . . . .]οντος κ[.]οτ̣[. . . . . 29 . . . .]
[. . . . . . 16 . . . . . . Ἀθέν]α̣ζε hο[. . .]μ[. . . . . 30 . . . .]
[. . . . . 21 . . . .] Ἀ̣θ̣έ[ν]εσ[ι . . . . 30 . . . .]
[. . . . . 21 . . . .]ˡ[. .]αυτ[. . . . . 31 . . . .]
[. . . . . 13 . . . . .]ο̣ι̣[. 4 . . h.]ι δὲ σ[. . . . . 34 . . . .]
[. . . . . 13 . . . . .]ιαν[. . 5 . .]ˡυʳ[. . . . . 34 . . . .]
[. . . . 10 . . . .] τ̣ριάκον[τα . . . . 39 . . . .]
[. . 6 . . . πρ]εσβευτὲς ἒ ε[. . . . . 40 . . . .]
[. . 6 . . . μ]εδὲν μέτε ἐνδε[. . . . . 38 . . . . τ]
[õν χσυ]μμάχον hότι ἂμ μὲ Ἀθε[ναίοις . . . . 29 . . . . ἄτ]
[ιμο]ς ἔστο καὶ τὰ χρέματα α[ὐτõ δεμόσια ἔστο τε͂ς τε θεõ τὸ ἐπιδέκατον· τὰ]
[ς] δὲ δίκας ἐ͂ναι Μιλεσίοις κα[. . . . . 35 . . . .]
δραχμ̣ὰς ἀπὸ τõν ἐπιδεκάτο[ν . . . . 32 . . . . τὰ]
δ̣ὲ πρυτανεῖα τιθέντον πρὸς [τὸς ἄρχοντας . . . . 23 . . . . hα]
[ι δ]ὲ δίκαι Ἀθένεσι ὄντον ἐν τ[. . . . . 30 . . . . Ἀνθεσ]
[τε]ριõνι καὶ Ἐλαφεβολιõνι· h[οι δὲ . . . . 32 . . . .]
[. .] νέμαντες καὶ κλερόσαντε[ς . . . . 34 . . . .]
[. . .]όντον δύο τõν ἀρχόντον κ[αὶ . . . . 22 . . . . καὶ hο μισθὸς δ]
[ιδό]σθο τοῖς δικαστε͂σιν ἐκ τ̣õ[ν πρυτανείον . . . . 24 . . . .]
[. . .] π̣αρεχόντον τὸ δικαστ[έριον . . . . 22 . . . . ἐν τοῖς μεσὶ]
[τοῖς] προερεμένο̣[ι]ς ἒ εὐθυν[όσθον . . . . 30 . . . .]

[... π]ρ̣ὸς τὸς ἄρχοντας τὸς Ἀθ[εναίον ....29............]
[..5..] Ἀθέναζε τοῖς ἐπιμελετ̣[ε͂σι ....31..........]
[..5..]αι καθάπερ πρὸ το͂ καὶ ἐμ̣[...........34...........]
[...7...]ς ἐπιμελόσθον hοι πέν[τε ....32..........]
[..5.. δι]καστέριον καθίζει κ[..........34..........]
[...7...] πορευομένοις ε͂ναι ε[..........34..........]
[..4.]ι[.. h]οι ἄρχοντες hοι Ἀθενα[ίον ....30..........]
[..] τελε͂[σθα]ι̣· τὰς δὲ hυπὲρ hεκατὸ[ν δραχμὰς ....25..........]
[. ἐ]ν στέλει̣ [κα]ὶ τοῖς φσεφίσμασ[ι ....32..........]
[..] μὲ διαφθεί[ρεν] μεδὲ κακοτεχν[ε͂ν ....11.....· ἐὰν δέ τις τούτον τι παρ]
α̣βαίνει, γραφαὶ [ὄ]ντον κατ' αὐτο͂ π[ρὸς τὸς ....26..........]
ται· ἐσαγόντον μ[ὲν αὐ]τὸν ἒ ἐς hένα [..........22..........· τιμάτο δὲ τὸ]
δ̣ικαστέριον hότι ἂγ χ̣[ρε͂]ι̣ παθε͂ν ἒ ἀ[ποτεῖσαι ....21.......... τὰ]
[φ]σεφίσματα τὰ Ἀθεναίο[ν δ]ε̣μευσα[..........31..........]
[.]χοσι λαβόντες· ἀποδόντ[ον δὲ h]ἐντ̣[ινα ....28..........]
σ̣ιο hε πόλις ἀποδότο τὲν τιμ[..........36..........]
καὶ τὸ λοιπὸν ἐπιγραφὰς μὲ πο[ιε͂ν ....31..........]
ς περὶ το͂ν χρεμάτον τε͂ς ἐσφορᾶ[ς ....30.......... κ]
α̣τεδικάσαντο ἀλλέλον hοι οἴκοι οἰ[κο͂ντες ....25..........]
[τ]ὲμ πόλιν hε͂χον ἒ ἄλλει τινὶ ζεμία[ι ....29..........]
[ἀν]απόμπιμα ε͂ναι το͂ι ὀφλόντι παρὰ τ[..........29..........]
[. ἀπ]ο̣δ̣ο͂ναι ἒ χρέματα ἒ ἀργύριον ἀπὸ [..........29..........]
[..5..] ἐπ' Εὐθύνο ἄρχοντος· hὸς δ' ἂμ μὲ [..........29..........]
[...8+...]ναι hοι πέντε hοι ἄρχοντες καὶ ἔχσεν[..........28+..........]
[...8....]κ̣ᵛ φανον δίκαι ὄντον Ἀθένε[σι ....26..........]
[....10....]ᵛ ἐναντία τοῖς Ἀθεναίον σ[..........27..........]
[.....12.....] hοι πρυτάνες hοι Μιλεσ[ίον ....24..........]
[.......15...... h]εκάτεροι τὲμ πόλιν [..........27..........]
[..7....]ο̣[.....11.....] Μ̣ιλεσίον τον h[..........27..........]
[..6...]εσχο̣[....11..... h]οι μὲν Ἀθε[ναῖοι ....22..........]
[..5.. ἐ]χσορκ̣[...8....]ε[..5..]ι[..]πει̣[..........27..........]
[...7... h]οι δὲ ἄ[λλοι Μι]λέσι̣[οι ....34..........]
[....9....]ορκό[ντον δ]ὲ hοι πέν̣[τε ....32..........]
[....9....] ἐόντο[ν πρὶ]ν ἂν ὀμόσε[ι ....31..........]
[....10....]ς ὄντο[ν Μι]λέτο hος ἂν σ[χ]ε̣͂ι̣ hε[..........25..........]
[....10....] ἐπιμελ[ό]σθον hόπος ἂν ἄριστ[α ....24..........]
[.4.. το͂ν Μιλ]εσίον ἒ [το͂]ν φρουρο͂ν κύριοι ὄ[ντον ....21..........]
[....10....] μέζονο[ς ἄ]χσ[ι]ος ε͂ι ζεμίας Ἀθε[ν..........23..........]
[..6... ἐπιβ]αλόντε[ς h]οπόσες ἂν δοκε͂ι ἄχσ[ιος ....21..........]
[...8.... ἐσφ]έρεσ⟨θ⟩[αι ἐ]ς τὸν δε͂μον hυπὸ το[..........24..........]

[. .⁵. . ἐφσεφ]ίσθαι αὐ̣[το]ῖς ἔτι εἴτε ἄλλο τι δ̣[. . . . . .²³. . . . .]
[. . . . .¹⁰. . . . .]οντες Μ[ιλέ]σιοι· ἐὰν δὲ σοφρονô[. . . . . .²³. . . . .]
[. . . . .¹⁰. . . . .]ṿ δέοντ[αι· π]ερὶ δὲ Ἀρνασô hε βο[λὲ . . . . .²². . . . .]
[. . . . . .¹¹. . . . .]ατ[. .⁶. . .]τον hόπος ἂν ἄρχοντ[αι . . . . .²¹. . . . .]
[. . . .⁹. . . . . h]ε βολ[ὲ τε̃ς φ]υλακε̃ς· τỗν δὲ φσεφ[ισ. . . . . .²². . . . .]
[. . .⁸. . . . .ος] ἂν ἐπιτ[ελε̃]ται hε βολὲ αὐτοκράτ[ορ ἔστο . . . . .¹⁷. . . . .]
[. .⁶. . . ἀποσ]τελάντο[ν τὸ] φρορίδε καὶ τὸς ἀ[. . . . . .²⁴. . . . .]
[. . . . .¹⁰. . . . .]σι τον ἐπ' [Εὐθ]ύνο ἄρχοντος ⟦— — — — — — — — — — — — *rasura:* traces visible— — —⟧
⟦— *rasura*— —⟧

Line 1: Meritt, who has also suggested (*Epigraphica Attica*, p. 144, n. 3) the possibility of [*Μι*]*λεσι̣*[*ον χσυνγ*]*γρ*[*αφαί*] on the analogy of the spelling in line 3. The error in correction would have been the same as in line 3 and the nu might have been squeezed in; there is no room for an additional evenly spaced letter, hence Meritt's [*Μι*]*λεσι̣*[*ον*]. In fact, the letters of the heading, measured on centers, give a horizontal *stoichos* of *ca* 0.037 m.; the distance from iota to gamma, as determined by the correct placement of fragments *a* and *b*, is *ca* 0.274 m. This allows about six and a half letters in the lacuna where we restore seven. Perhaps the chi was originally absent.

Lines 2–3: [*ἔδοχσεν*] *τε̃ι βολε̃ι κα*[*ὶ τỗι δέμοι*] Koumanoudes. [— — —*ὶς ἐπρ*]*υτάν*[*ευε, Εὐκλε̃ς ἐγραμμάτευε*] Kirchhoff (*I.G.*, I, *Suppl.*, no. 22*a*); [*Κεκροπὶς ἐπρ*]*υτάν*[*ευε*, . .⁶. . . *ἐγραμμάτ* | *ευε*, *'Ονέτ*]*ορ* Woodhead, following P. Haggard, *The Secretaries of the Athenian Boulê in the Fifth Century B.C.*, p. 25; [*'Ερεχθεὶς ἐπρ*]*υτάν*[*ευε, Λέον ἐγραμμάτευ*|*ε, Εὐφράν*]*ορ* Mattingly, *Historia*, XII (1963), pp. 265–66. We do not venture a restoration. Mattingly piles hypothesis on hypothesis in order to restore Erechtheis for the sake of supporting his case for dating the inscription in the last prytany of 426/5 B.C. But, if he restores Euphranor, he should at least, on his own evidence, restore Antiochis rather than Erechtheis. Two, probably three, men of this name are attested for the former tribe, only one for the latter; the casualty in line 45 (col. I) of *I.G.*, I², 950, which has anathyrosis on the left, cited by Mattingly as from Erechtheis (tribe I), cannot be from that tribe; he is most likely from Antiochis (X), possibly from Aiantis (IX). See Bradeen, *Class. Quart.*, N.S. XIX (1969), pp. 147–48.

Line 3: [Εὔθυνος ἐ̃ρχε] Hiller; cf. lines 61 and 86. [τάδε hοι χ]συνγγρα[φε̃ς χσυνέγραφσαν] Oliver, citing Foucart, *B.C.H.*, IV (1880), p. 251, who in fact deemed the first gamma a mason's error for epsilon and misjudged the length of the lacuna ([τάδε οἱ ξυγγραφη̃ς] ξυν⟨έ⟩γρα[ψαν]); see *I.G.*, I², 76, 3–4. The restorations are probably correct. In the two appearances of Euthynos the context is not clear enough to show that the reference is to this decree. Line 61 may well look back to some previous action (see the commentary), which could, of course, have been in the same year. Pedieus, archon in 449/8, remains a candidate for line 3 but the appearance of a garrison in Miletos makes a date after the Peace of Kallias (spring 449) unlikely; see Meritt and Wade-Gery, *J.H.S.*, LXXXIII (1963), p. 102.

Lines 3–4: [τε|λε̃ν τὰ ν]ομιζόμενα Meritt; [συντελέσαι | μὲν τὰ ν]ομιζόμενα το[ι̃ς θεοι̃ς] Hiller. [hελέσθαι δ]ὲ πέντε ἄν[δρας τὸν δε̃μον] Kirchhoff. Although the sense is clear and Kirchhoff's hελέσθαι has been accepted by all subsequent editors, the necessity of restoring an aspirate alone in its *stoichos* in this part of the inscription makes the reading suspect. We therefore prefer hαιρε̃σθαι; this form is used in *A.T.L.*, II, D8, 39 (*I.G.*, I², 65).

Lines 4–5: [ἐχς hαπ|άντον] Oliver; [ἐχς Ἀθεναίον hαπάντον] Kirchhoff; [ἐχς Ἀθεναίον π|άντον] Hiller.

Line 5: [hυπὲρ τριάκοντα ἔτε] γεγονότα̣[ς] Kirchner (*I.G.*, I², 22); ḥ[υπέρ] Oliver; ḥ[υπὲρ πεντέκοντα ἔτε] Mattingly, *Class. Quart.*, N.S. XVI (1966), p. 190; ụ̔[πέρ] BM. On the stone there is an eroded area, similar to others in this fragment, which seems to follow the left side of upsilon. The mark that Oliver took as the left hasta of *H* is much too shallow and continues up into the letter above; see Plate VII. For fifty as an age-limit see *A.T.L.*, II, D3, line 17 (*I.G.*, I², 57), and D12 (Plutarch, *Pericles*, 17).

Lines 5–6: [ἐχσομοσίαν δὲ μὲ ἐ͂να|ι τούτοις] West; [αὐτο͜ῖς] Oliver; cf. *S.E.G.*, X, 24, line 14.

Line 6: [μ]εδὲ ἀνθαι[ρε͂σθαι ἄλλεν ἀρ]χέν Hiller; ἀνθ⟨α⟩ί[ρεσιν, τούτος δὲ ἄρ]χεν West; the stone shows ΑΝΘΛΙ. Sufficient of the noun is preserved to make it highly probable that details of the election are still being treated. In the lacuna a shift is made to the duties of the Five. West's restoration, with its awkward τούτος, while rather general, seems unavoidable. Hiller's ἀνθαι[ρε͂σθαι ἄλλεν ἀρ]χέν is too short. Lines 6–9 apparently deal with some of these duties but the text is so fragmentary that we do not venture restoration. One must always keep in mind the sudden changes in subject-matter possible in Attic decrees; *A.T.L.*, II, D10 (*I.G.*, I², 11, Regulations for Erythrai), is an apposite example, especially lines 8–9. The *syngrapheis*, we infer, had agenda composed at least in part of specific questions, which they settled one by one.

Lines 6–7: συν[βολεύεν αὐτὸς καὶ συμπ|ράττεν τ]οῖς Oliver; συν[βολεύεν το͂ι τε αἰσυμνέ|τει καὶ τ]οῖς Woodhead. Both supplements rest on the belief that the *prosetairoi* are mentioned in line 7 (*q.v.*). We doubt that the letter following συν- was beta, since the normal change of nu to mu occurs in the text without exception (lines 27, 58, 61, 66).

Line 7: [τ]οῖς προσε[ταίροις] Hiller; [τ]οῖς προσε[ταίρο͜ις μολπο͂ν κα]ὶ μετὰ το͂ α̣ἰ̣[συμνέτο] Oliver; προσερ̣[BM. The removal of fragment *a* from the plaster disclosed the remains of a left-hand upright at the break, as previously indicated by Koumanoudes, Ἀθήναιον, V (1876), p. 167; see Plate VII. The letter looks most like rho but might be kappa (προσέκ̣[εν ἐς Μίλετον κα]ί?). With the *prosetairoi* eliminated, the subject-matter of this passage becomes even less clear.

Line 8: [Ἀθ]ένεσι (?) Kirchhoff. This reading has been generally accepted but the possibility of a dative plural feminine, especially of the middle or passive participle, cannot be ignored; the context is apparently naval. [στρατε]γὸς τὸς Μιλ[εσίον] Koumanoudes; καὶ [τ]ὸ[ς στρατε]γός Hiller; [τ]ὸ[ς hὲχς(?) στρατε]γός Oliver, which fits the spacing and is possible; the number of generals is unknown but Miletos had six tribes.

Line 9: [Μιλ]εσίον το[---ν]όμος δέκα το[---] Kirchhoff;]ος δεκατο[Koumanoudes; τὸ[ς . . . ἀγ]ογὸς δέκα το[Hiller. το[σ . . . .⁹. . . .]γος δὲ κατο Woodhead. The first omicron on fragment *b* is not certain, but there seem to be traces of its bottom at the break; this makes us hesitant to restore τὸ[ς δὲ στρατε]γὸς δέκα τὸ[ς Ἀθεναίον], which would fit well with what follows.

Lines 10–23: This section, which mentions triremes (or trierarchs), transports, four obols in pay, and soldiers, is taken as a rule as arranging for Milesian military aid to Athens; see Oliver, pp. 190–191; *A.T.L.*, III, p. 256; Mattingly, *Historia*, X (1961), p. 176, and *Class. Quart.*, N.S. XVI (1966), pp. 189–90, and *A.S.&I.*, p. 208; Meritt and Wade-Gery, *J.H.S.*, LXXXIII (1963), p. 101. The assumption depends upon the appearance of Ἀθέναζε three times (lines 15, 16, 19). The context, however, is so broken that we cannot even be sure that the military section continues beyond line 15. The passage could better be understood as referring to details of the transportation of the new board and the reorganization of the garrison; so D. M. Lewis, *B.S.A.*, XLIX (1954), p. 24, n. 19, and Bengtson, *op. cit.*, p. 64. The four obols in pay ought surely to be ascribed to the Athenians. See also line 85, which seems to look back to the despatch of military forces.

Line 10: τριέ[ρον καὶ] ṭôν στρατιοṭίḍ[ον] Hiller, which does not fill the lacuna; other possibilities are τριέṛ[ον hὲχς καί] and τριερ̣[άρχος τὸς] ṭôν (*West*).

Line 11: hόπλα Koumanoudes. Since the omicron shows no crowding, it is likely that the *daseia* was here omitted.

Line 12: δὲ του Koumanoudes.

Line 13: ὀβο[λ]ός Koumanoudes; [φέρεν hέκαστον τέ]τταρας ὀβο[λὸ]ς π[αρὰ τôν κολακρετôν?] Oliver, from *S.E.G.*, X, 24, lines 8–9.

Line 14:]ον hεκάστο [τô] σόμ[ατος] Hiller; the stone has HEKΛ̣ΑΤO.

Line 15: [Ἀθέν]αζε Koumanoudes. στρ[α]τιό[ταις] Koumanoudes; στ[ρα]τιό[τεσι] Kirchhoff.

Line 16: [Ἀθέ]ναζε Koumanoudes. δ' ἄ[ν] Kirchhoff.

Line 17: hοπόσα Koumanoudes.

Line 19: [Ἀθέν]αζ[ε] *ho* Koumanoudes; *ho*[ι δὲ] *M*[ιλέσιοι] is possible.

Line 20: [---]ε[.]εσ[---] *priores*; Ἀ̣θ̣έ[ν]εσ[ι] BM. We see the apex and right side of alpha, the top of theta (or omicron).

Line 22: ιδες Hiller; ιδε Oliver; the crowded iota makes [*ho*]ι or [*hα*]ι obligatory.

Line 23: IYΓ Koumanoudes; ˡYΓ̣ Hiller; *h̥υπ* Oliver. In the first space the right-hand vertical could be part of nu or the *daseia*; absence of crowding favors nu. The third letter is epsilon or pi.

Lines 24–28: By line 24 the subject-matter has obviously changed. Now we meet an ambassador, the allies, prohibitions, and legal penalties. West and Oliver take these together and assume that these clauses limit any independent or anti-Athenian action by Miletos' representative in the assembly of the allies. But the surviving text is too fragmentary: the ambassador may not be Milesian, the potential miscreants are not necessarily Milesians alone, and we think it unlikely that the allied synods were still meeting (cf. *A.T.L.*, III, pp. 138–41). One might expect designation of those Milesians, presumably supporters of the late revolt, who are subject to trial. Perhaps the ambassador was one of a number of officials so subject, although lines 26–27 scarcely fit this sense. On the other hand, the prohibitions and penalties more probably look to the future.

Line 26: [μ]εδέν Koumanoudes.

Lines 26–27: ἐνδε[ές] Hiller; some form of ἐνδείκνυμι is also possible. [χσυ]μμάχον Koumanoudes. μέτε ἐνδέ[χεται τοῦτο ἒ φσεφον εἴπει ἐν τοι χσυνεδρίοι τοι τ|ον χσυ]μμάχον West; μέτε ἐνδέ[χεσθαι αὐτὸν φσεφον εἰπεν ἐν τοῖ χσυνεδρίοι τοι τ|ον χσυ]μμάχον Oliver.

Line 27: Ἀθε[ναίοις ἐπιτέδειον ἐι· ἐὰν δέ τι τούτον ποιει] Oliver. This may be right and would fit the *stoichedon* pattern if we read ποει. There are, however, other possibilities, *e.g.*, Ἀθε[ναίοις δοκει ἀγαθόν· hόστις δ' ἂν τοῦτο ποιει].

Lines 27–28: [ἄτ|ιμο]ς ἔστο καὶ τὰ χρέματα α[ὐτο δεμόσια] Koumanoudes; α[ὐτο δεμόσια ἔστο καὶ τες θεο τὸ ἐπιδέκατον] Meritt. The sense is certain; the substitution of τε for καί is necessitated by the length of line.

Lines 28–51: There is no doubt that this section establishes a procedure for trials of Milesians at Athens; its relationship with what precedes, however, is obscure and there are questions about the types of cases involved. Oliver understood lines 28–40 as pertaining to "disputes over the matters regulated or indicated in the preceding paragraph" (p. 191), which we think may be partially right, and concluded that they "largely concerned the *phoros*" (p. 192), which we think most unlikely. He found parallels in the assessment-decree of 425/4 B.C. (*A.T.L.*, II, A9) and the decree of 426/5 appointing *eklogeis* (*A.T.L.*, II, D8), drawing upon both for his restoration. Mattingly and, to an extent, Meritt and Wade-Gery apparently concur (*loc. cit.*). We believe that the court envisaged and indeed the whole document have nothing to do with *phoros*; there is no hint extant. Oliver then argued that lines 45–51 regulated procedure in private cases (p. 194) and that, after a change of subject-matter, the aorists (lines 52–54) imply a decision on some private issue (p. 198).

Our view, to which we shall return in the commentary, is that in lines 28–40 we are dealing with the establishment and functioning of a special court to try Milesians in Athens. The defendants may be those already accused of transgression or those who may be charged in the future.[20] Mention of the ἐπιδέκατον in line 30 suggests that the crimes alleged are serious ones, the penalties for which are ἀτιμία and confiscation of property (see lines 27–28, where the restoration is convincing). Assessment of the ἐπιδέκατον is in Athens connected with ἀτιμία and confiscation of property in *A.T.L.*, II, D14, §3 (the decree of Klearchos about coinage), *I.G.*, I², 39, 33–36 (*A.T.L.*, II, D17; the fraction goes to Olympian Zeus), *I.G.*, I², 45, 23–25 (the colony to Brea), *A.T.L.*, II, A9, 32–33, Andokides, I, 96 (in a quoted decree), Plutarch, *Moralia*, 834A (*Vit. X Orat.*; added to a decree, purportedly of 411/0), Xenophon, *Hell.*, I, 7, 10. The only exception[21] is in Demosthenes, 43, 71 (a quoted *lex*), where the ἐπιδέκατον is to come from the fine imposed on one who steals an olive tree and to be given to Athena, perhaps because the olive was deemed to be Athena's tree. Upon this single instance we do not base a presumption that the ἐπιδέκατον was computed on fines. Rather, we incline

[20] According to Gomme, *Commentary*, I, p. 350, "arrangements were made for the trial of further cases in which 'treason' was suspected," *i.e.*, the δίκαι of line 29 are specific in that they relate to the crimes and penalties just mentioned.

[21] Lines 5–6 of *I.G.*, I², 28*a* (*S.E.G.*, X, 23) are restored as follows by Wilhelm (*Attische Urkunden*, IV, *Sitzungsb. Ak. Wien*, 217, 5 [1939], no. 21, pp. 19–21):

πρυτ[ανεῖα δὲ μὲ τελε͂]
[ν πλ]ὲν πέντε δραχμ[ὰς μεδὲ τἀπιδέκ]
[ατα?]

Even apart from our disapproval of the crasis and the plural number, this cannot be right. The ἐπιδέκατον in Athens has nothing to do with the litigants and their fees; it is a percentage dedicated to a deity, generally Athena, of a fine or, more often, of the proceeds of confiscated property. Wilhelm seeks support from late texts from Peparethos (*I.G.*, XII, 8, 640, line 25), Stymphalos (*I.G.*, V, 2, 357, line 58), and Tauromenion (*I.G.*, XIV, 432, lines 8–9), *e.g.*: δεδόσθαι δ[ὲ α]ὐτῶι καὶ γῆς καὶ οἰκίας ἔγκτησιν καὶ προ[δ]ικίαν ἄνευ ἐπιδεκάτων (Peparethos). In all these passages the ἐπιδέκατα are demonstrably what the Athenians called πρυτανεῖα, "court-fees." Never do πρυτανεῖα and ἐπιδέκατα appear together as parallel fees, as Wilhelm restores *I.G.*, I², 28*a*. In place of [μεδὲ τἀπιδέκατα] we propose [τὸν γραφσάμενον], which supplies a subject for the infinitive. The restoration τά τε πρυτανεῖα καὶ τ[ὰ ἐπιδέκατα?] in *I.G.*, II², 179, line 15 must also be rejected.

to the view that levying of the *ἐπιδέκατον* was restricted to cases involving *ἀτιμία* and sacrilege.

These cases, then, are major, *e.g.*, treason. Yet the complexity of the machinery, the need for two archons with colleagues (line 35), and the apparent size of the jury (lines 33–34 with commentary) suggest that much business was anticipated, which is surprising. The ringleaders of the revolt must surely have been dealt with already and one would scarcely expect a great many cases of such importance in the future.

In line 46 *τὰς δὲ hυπὲρ hεκατὸ[ν δραχμάς]* must be right; *i.e.*, we are now considering cases in which either the penalties are fines or the property involved is given a monetary value. In other words we have passed from the capital cases that threaten *ἀτιμία* to a different type of litigation, some of which is to be heard in Miletos. Where the transition occurs is not easy to determine. We suspect that it should be sought in lines 40–41, although *πορευομένοις* (line 44) is a disturbing element; very probably, in lines 40–46, the cases are commercial, in which Milesians and Athenians are litigants.

Provision for publication (lines 46–47) is now followed by a declaration that the Milesians henceforth must respect the decrees of the Athenians; the procedure to be adopted in the event of transgression is specified in detail.

In our study of lines 28–51 we have concluded that Oliver often comes very close in his restorations to what the original text must have been and we have not hesitated to borrow from him, making slight adjustments to maintain the length of line at 58 letters.

Lines 28–30: [*τὰ*|*ς*] *δέ* Koumanoudes. *κα*[*τα*––] Hiller; *κα*[*θάπερ*] *West*, Oliver; *κα*[*θάπερ Ἀθεναίοις καὶ χιλίας*] BM. [*ἀπὸ τô ταλάντο*] | *δραχμὰς ἀπὸ τôν ἐπιδεκάτο*[*ν ἐ̑ναι hιερὰς τôι Ἀπόλλονι τôι ἐν Διδύμοις*] West. West's restoration is probably right and fits the line if we read *hιεράς* in the normal style. From what is preserved we judge that provision is being made for sharing

Athena's portion (the ἐπιδέκατα) of Milesian confiscations with Apollo at Didyma (*pace* Wilamowitz, *Arist. u. Ath.*, I, p. 223, n. 72; as the trials are to be held in Athens it is hardly credible that Athena would not receive the major share). For the amount to be surrendered we should expect 100 or 1000 drachmai on the talent; we prefer the latter, for 100 drachmai would most likely be expressed as μνᾶ (see *A.T.L.*, II, List 1, line 3; 33, line 7; 34, line 7). The division of the ἐπιδέκατον would be one of the few differences in a trial of a Milesian in Athens from that of an Athenian. We believe that this section, dealing with trials of Milesians in Athens, most logically began with a general statement to the effect that the latter would be tried like Athenians, followed by stipulation of the necessary exceptions in detail. For our [Ἀθεναίοις καί] we might read [Ἀθεναίοις πλέν].

Lines 30–31: [δ]έ Koumanoudes. πρὸς [τὸς ἄρχοντας τὸς Ἀθεναίον] Lipsius, *Att. Recht*, III, p. 827, n. 83; πρὸς [τὸν πολέμαρχον?] Hiller; πρὸς [τὸς ἄρχοντας τὸς Ἀθεναίον hένει καὶ νέαι] Oliver; [τὸς Ἀθεναίον τὸς ἐν Μιλέτοι] BM. Oliver's text, which combines Lipsius' and his own restorations, may be right; it requires that one *daseia* in the line occupy a whole *stoichos*, which is perhaps contrary to the mason's practice in this area. There remains, however, a problem; this version does not make clear who the *archontes* are, those in Athens or those in Miletos. Yet this is what we should expect to be specified here; the Milesians should know where to pay their court-fees. We believe that they were to pay in Miletos to the Athenian officials there. The context indicates in lines 39 and 45, where *archontes* are designated as Athenian, that they are serving in Miletos; and the Five are called *archontes* in line 62. The *archontes* named without qualification in line 35 must be members of the regular Athenian board.

Lines 31–33: [hα|ι δ]έ Koumanoudes. [Ἀνθεσ|τε]ριõνι Kirchhoff; ἐν τ[οῖς μεσὶ Ποσιδειõνι καὶ Γαμελιõνι καὶ Ἀνθεσ | τε]ριõνι Oliver; ἐν τ[ε̃ι ἐλιαίαι ἐν τοῖς μεσὶ Γαμελιõνι καὶ Ἀνθεσ | τε]ριõνι BM. Oliver's restoration is too long by one letter; his defense for the inclusion of Posideion rests mainly on his assumption that this passage deals with assessment-cases (p. 193). This sentence deals with time and place and should be more specific than merely *Ἀθένεσι*. Oliver restored an allusion to the heliaia in line 34; it is more appropriate here.

Lines 33–34: *h*[οι δ' ἄρχοντες δικαστὰς καθιστάντον, κατὰ φυλ|ὰς] ṿέμαντες καὶ κλερόσαντε[ς αὐτὸς ἐν τε̑ι ἐλιαίαι] Oliver. Apart from the placement of the heliaia here, there are two other problems in the restoration. First is the elision *hοι* δ' ἄρχοντες: on the extant stone elision of δέ occurs only before ἄν (lines 16, 61), otherwise (lines 70, 81) δέ before a vowel retains its epsilon. Second, there is no mention of the number of jurors. The number, of course, is unknown but, with two archons cited below, we might expect a substantial body. In *A.T.L.*, II, A9 (line 16), the new court comprises 1,000 men. In fact, by following the text of A9, we can produce a supplement that just fits our present requirements: *h*[οι δὲ νομοθέται (?) καθιστάντον χιλίος δικαστ|ὰς] νέμαντες καὶ κλερόσαντε[ς αὐτὸς κατὰ φυλάς]. *Νομοθέται* may not be the correct noun; Kahrstedt (*Gött. gel. Anz.* [1935], p. 51, and *Klio*, XXXI [1938], p. 9) objected to its restoration by Meritt and West in A9 and it is true that, in its fourth-century sense, it is not suitable here. Nonetheless, both here and in A9 a nine-letter noun fits in similar contexts. Who drew the jurors in the fifth century we do not know; but it was a group designated by a nine-letter noun ending in -θέται. These may have been νομοθέται, with functions different from those of the next century, or they may have been minor officials of whom we have no record (*e.g.*, δικαθέται?).

Lines 34–35: [ἐ|σαγ]όντον Wilamowitz, *Arist. u. Ath.*, I, p. 223, n. 72; [καὶ τὰς δίκας ταύτας ἐ|σαγ]όντον δύο τον̑ ἀρχόντον κ[αθάπερ τὰς ἄλλας τον̑ ἐλιαστον̑] Oliver, who depended upon A9, lines 13–14, although he preferred Wilamowitz's ἐσαγόντον to ἀνακρινάντον. The latter suits better our restoration of the previous sentence. The plural ending of the verb forces us to read the kappa of line 35 as part of καί, as δύο τôν ἀρχόντον alone demands a dual verb; see Meisterhans-Schwyzer, p. 199. Since the end of the line may be restored with reasonable security, [ho δὲ μισθὸς δ] or [καὶ ho μισθὸς δ], the length of the lacuna after κ[αί] must be twenty-three or twenty-two *stoichoi*. These should conceal the officials who are to assist the two archons. The documented possibilities are εἰσαγωγεῖς, known from A9, lines 7, 12, 59–60, and restored in D7, line 71, and line 37 of our document by Oliver, and ἐπιμεληταί, known from D8, lines 38 ff., and from line 40 below. Their appearance in line 40 makes them more likely here. Little is known of the office, of which there has been recent discussion. Mattingly (*Historia*, X [1961], p. 177) claimed that it was established in 426/5 by D8; Meritt and Wade-Gery (*J.H.S.*, LXXXIII [1963], p. 102) rightly reject this; they conclude "that the *epimeletai* were not a standing board, but one that was appointed from time to time" that seemed "to take care of punishable offences (*graphai* rather than *diadikasiai*) in connexion with public matters such as tribute." We do not think, however, that the text of D8 necessarily implies that *epimeletai*, dealing with trials, were not a standing board; it sets up *epimeletai* τô[ν ἄλλον δικôν τôν περὶ] τôν Ἀθεναίον χρεμάτον, which could well mean only that extra officials of this class are needed because of the new regulations. *Epimeletes*, indeed, is such a general term (cf. Aristotle, *Ath. Pol.*, 43, 1: ἐπιμεληταὶ τῶν κρηνῶν; *I.G.*, II², 1672, line 246: τῶν μυστηρίων; 1629, line 179: τῶν νεωρίων) that it needs definition, at least on first mention. A group that helped and supplemented the archons in judicial matters should be called ἐπιμεληταὶ τῶν δικῶν. Hence we can now restore [hοι ἐπιμελεταὶ hοι τôν δικôν καὶ ho μισθός]. If this is judged tenuous, we still insist that the lacuna contained a designation of those who, along with the two archons, were involved in the trials.

Lines 35–36: [δ|ιδό]σθο Kirchhoff; [ho δὲ μισθὸς δ|ιδό]σθο Wilamowitz; [καὶ ho μισθός] (or [ho δέ]) BM. ἐκ τ[ôν πρυτανείον]

Oliver; cf. [Xen.], I, 16; *I.G.*, II², 179, lines 13–15. We note that this clause, logically, is out of order; in sense it belongs after the selection of the jurors.

Lines 36–37: [καὶ τοῖς πρέσβεσιν τοῖς Μιλεσ|ίον π]αρεχόντον Oliver (with the *phoros* in mind); [καὶ τοῖς ἐκ Μιλέτο πορευομέν|οις] π̣αρεχόντον BM; another possibility is [τοῖς ἐπὶ δίκεν (or δίκας) πορευομέν|οις].

Line 37: δικασ[τέριον] Koumanoudes; δικαστ[έριον πλε̑ρες] Wilamowitz; δικαστ[έριον hοι ἄρχοντες καὶ hοι ἐσαγογε̑ς] Oliver; δκιαστ[έριον ἐπάναγκες hοι ἀεὶ ἄρχοντες] BM. Oliver's version is too long. The present tenses in this passage imply an annual procedure, which supports ἀεί.

Lines 37–38: [ἐν τοῖς μεσὶ | τοῖς] προερεμένοις Wilamowitz.

Line 38: εὐθυν[έσθο *vel* όσθον] Kirchhoff; εὐθυν[όσθον χιλίασι δραχμε̑σι] Hiller; εὐθυν[έσθο μυρίασι (?) δραχμε̑σιν hέκαστος αὐτο̑ν] Oliver. Hiller's supplement is more credible; Oliver's allows only six letter-spaces before the prepositional phrase in line 39, hardly enough for the introduction of a new subject.

Lines 38–40: This passage turns to the details of procedure in Miletos for Milesians who are to be tried in Athens. The Athenian officials in Miletos seem to be responsible for sending something (*e.g.*, τὰ πρυτανεῖα) and perhaps someone (*e.g.*, the defendants) to Athens.

Lines 38–39: [π]ρὸς τὸς ἄρχοντας τὸς Ἀθεν[αίον] Koumanoudes; [hόταν δέ τις πρυταν|εῖα π]ρ̣ὸς τὸς ἄρχον̇τας τὸς Ἀθ[εναίον τίθει] BM.

Line 40: ἐπιμελε[ταῖς] Koumanoudes; ἐπιμελετ[ε̑σι] Kirchhoff.

Lines 40–46: We place the change from one type of case to another in line 40. We venture no restoration of these fragmentary lines. Our conception of the sense is as follows: certain trials are to take place in Miletos as before, the Athenian officials in Miletos are to see that stipulated procedures are respected (*e.g.*, that jurors are appointed? *anakriseis* occur?), the convening of a court is mentioned. We find πορευομένοις baffling; perhaps it refers to Athenians who may travel to Miletos. If so, these cases are *δίκαι ἀπὸ ξυμβολῶν*.[22] In line 45 the Athenian archons in Miletos are responsible for some duty and in the next line *τελε̑[σθα]ι̣* probably refers to a payment (of a fine? of a judgment?). Whenever more than 100 drachmai are at stake, the case may be appealed to Athens (line 46: [*ἐκκλέτος*]). The best explanation of the whole passage is that commercial cases involving both Athenians and Milesians are the subject. The *syngrapheis* enact that such cases are to be heard as before but the Athenian archons in Miletos are to take particular care of Athenian interests and there is to be the right of appeal to Athens. It is also possible that important cases involving only Milesians may be appealed to Athens.

Line 41: *ἐμ* [*Μιλέτοι* (?)] Wilamowitz.

Line 42: *πέν*[*τε*] Kirchhoff.

Line 43: [*δι*]*καστέριον* Koumanoudes.

Lines 43–44: [*τοῖς ἐπὶ τ*|*ὰς δίκας* (?)] *πορευομένοις* Oliver.

Line 45: [*h*]*οι ἄρχοντες hοι Ἀθενα*[*ίον*] Koumanoudes. There is no sign of crowding in [*h*]*οι*.

Line 46: *τ̣ελέσ*[*θα*]*ι̣* Oliver; *τελε̑*[*σθα*]*ι̣* BM. *hυπὲρ hεκατὸ*[*ν δραχμάς*] Kirchhoff. [*ἐκκλέτος ἐ̑ναι*] Oliver (cf. *I.G.*, II², 111, lines 73–75).

Lines 46–47: [*ταῦτα δ' ἀναγράφσα*|*ι ἐ*]*ν στέλει̣,* [*κα*]*ί* Oliver; [*ταῦτα δὲ γράφσα*|*ι ἐ*]*ν* BM (cf. *I.G.*, I², 45, line 17). Oliver's text does not fit the available space and the elision is unlikely; see on lines 33–34 above.

Lines 47–48: *φσεφίσμασ*[*ι τοῖς Ἀθεναίον αἰεὶ χρε̑σθαι τὸς Μιλεσίος κ*|*αὶ*] *μὲ διαφθε̣ί̣*[*ρεν*] *μεδέ* Oliver. The sense must be right and we make slight changes to accord with the length of line: *φσεφίσμασ*[*ι τοῖς Ἀθεναίον ἀεὶ πείθεσθαι Μιλεσίος κ*|*αί*]. Oliver assumes that the decrees here mentioned are "special decrees issued from time to time, concerning chiefly the

[22] Hopper, *J.H.S.*, LXIII (1943), pp. 49–50, because of the word *ἐπιδεκάτο*[*ν*] in line 30, denies that these are *δίκαι ἀπὸ ξυμβολῶν*; but he does not recognize that the legal phraseology in lines 30–65 applies to more than one type of case.

commercial relations between members of the empire" (p. 196). The context, however, strongly favors a wider interpretation, namely, that these are all Athenian decrees about the Milesians as well as those regulating the allies; see Meiggs, *J.H.S.*, LXIII (1943), p. 26.

Lines 48–49: κακοτεχν[ε͂ν hόπος μὲ κύρια ἔσται. ἐὰν δέ τις ταῦτα παρ|α]βαίνει Oliver. The sense must be close to the original, but the formula with παραβαίνω is normally τούτων τι rather than ταῦτα (cf. *I.G.*, I², 15, lines 41–42; 59, lines 23–24; 73, line 16; 76, lines 57–58). We therefore read: κακοτεχν[ε͂ν hόπος ἂν λυθε͂ι· ἐὰν δέ τις τούτον τι παρ|]α̣βαίνει.

Lines 49–51: [hότι χρὲ] παθε͂ν ἒ ἀ[ποτῖσαι] Koumanoudes; γραφαὶ [ὄ]ντον κατ' αὐτõ π[ρὸς τὸς θ̣εσμοθέτας Ἀθένεσι, hοι δὲ θεσμοθέ]|ται ἐσαγόντον μ[ὲν αὐ]τὸν ἒ ἐς hένα [καὶ διακοσίος ἒ τετρακοσίος· τιμάτο δὲ τὸ | δ]ικαστέριον hότι [ἂν] χ̣[ρε͂ι] παθε͂ν ἒ ἀ[ποτεῖσαι] Oliver; π[ροδοσίας πρὸς τὸς ἐπιμελετάς· hοι δ' ἐπιμελε]|ταί Mattingly, *Historia*, X (1961), p. 177. For the lacuna in line 49 Oliver's restoration is too long by two letters, Mattingly's, apart from an objectionable elision, by four. It is impossible to decide epigraphically whether *thesmothetai* or *epimeletai* belong in lines 49–50; but the persons before whom the indictments are laid (π[ρὸς---]) should be those who refer (ἐσαγόντον) the accused. These are unlikely to be *thesmothetai*, who are, after all, part of the board of archons, whom we are inclined to restore in line 50. For these reasons we propose π[ρὸς τὸς ἐπιμελετὰς εὐθύς]. The last sentence of Oliver's restoration is formulaic and probably right; we are thus left with a lacuna of twenty-two letter-spaces after ἐς hένα. Oliver's version, which, at first glance, seems attractive, is derived from Aristotle, *Ath. Pol.*, 53, 3: οἱ δὲ παραλαβόντες εἰσάγουσιν εἰς τὸ δικαστήριον, τὰ μὲν ἐντὸς χιλίων εἰς ἕνα καὶ διακοσίους, τὰ δ' ὑπὲρ χιλίας εἰς ἕνα καὶ τετρακοσίους. But we doubt whether ἒ ἐς hένα καὶ διακοσίος ἒ τετρακοσίος can mean "either to the 201 or to the 401." Moreover, the phrase is too long for the space. Aristotle is describing cases of appeal from the *diaitetai* in civil actions after several changes in the system of courts, whereas our context clearly indicates criminal cases. In fact, very little is known of the numbers of dikasts in juries in the fifth century. This would be the first hint that an odd number might be used (see Lipsius, *op. cit.*, I, pp. 134–139; Bonner and Smith, *The Administration of Justice from Homer to Aristotle*, I [Chicago, 1930], pp. 224–48); panels seem usually to have been of five hundred or multiples thereof. It is not easy to imagine why juries of two different sizes should be mentioned here; in fact, it is not easy to comprehend why a choice is offered at all. Understanding is further complicated by the particle μ[έν], which anticipates an answering δέ; that is, [*hοι* ἐπιμελε]ταί (δέ is the normal transitional particle) ἐσαγόντον stands in contrast to [τιμάτο τὸ] δικαστέριον. A similar procedure is enacted in the Decree of Kleinias (*A.T.L.*, II, D7, lines 33–39), where the *prytaneis* receive the indictment and refer the defendant to the Boule, the Boule decide guilt or innocence, the *heliaia* assess the penalty. In the present text the *epimeletai* (?) receive the indictment and then refer the indictment to A or B, the court assesses the penalty. Apparently, A and B have the responsiblity of deciding guilt or innocence, although this duty cannot, because of limitations of space, be envisaged as included in the document. It remains to identify A and B. The presence of *h*ένα shows that A is masculine. We cannot discover a suitable body and we conclude that we are dealing with a person, even though we have some qualms about the syntax of εἰσάγειν εἴς τινα. We suggest, tentatively, ἐς *h*ένα [τὸν ἀρχόντον] and we add [ἒ ἐς τὲμ βολέν], which precisely fits the remaining space. This implies that an archon had the power to make judicial decisions. If this were true, it would affect current ideas about the development of Athenian judicial procedure.[23]

[23] Wade-Gery, *Essays*, pp. 180–200, especially 181–86, in a study of *I.G.*, I², 16, the judicial treaty with Phaselis, interprets παρ[ὰ τῶι πο]λεμάρχωι (lines 9–10) as "at the Polemarch's tribunal," and proposes that certain magistrates could give

Our lingering doubts about the appropriateness of ἔ . . . [ἔ] in line 50, a construction that gives a startling choice to magistrates ([ἐπιμελε]ταί), tempt us to welcome a radical solution, which we here submit. The first draft of line 50 (drawn in chalk) read: TAIEϟAΛONTONMENAYTONEIϟENA. The mason, instructed to correct the Ionicisms, erased IϟE and substituted EϟHE. He should, of course, have erased the epsilon preceding iota. Thus four letters were cut in three *stoichoi*, as the stone demonstrably shows, two Ionicisms were eliminated, and a redundant epsilon was carelessly left in the text. The clause would read: [*hοι δὲ ἐπιμελε]ταὶ ἐσαγόντον μ[ὲν αὐ]τὸν {ε} ἐς hένα [τôν ἀρχόντον πέντε hεμερôν]* (or [*δέκα hεμερôν*]).

Lines 51–61: In the middle of line 51 there must be a complete change of subject as the *syngrapheis* turn to specific problems and questions raised by the recent revolt (see Oliver, p. 198). This is demonstrated not only by the context but also by the aorists in lines 52, 53, 54, 57, 59 and 60, in contrast to the presents used earlier. In general, we believe, this section deals with compensation for victims of the revolt. Restoration of the text is made most difficult by the cryptic nature of replies to questions of this type in Attic decrees; cf., *e.g.*, *I.G.*, I², 39, lines 52–57.

Lines 51–53: [δ]εμευσα Koumanoudes; [*τοῖς*] *ἐν τ*[*έλει*] West; [*ἐὰν δέ τις φανêι διαφθείρας τὰ* | *φ*]*σεφίσματα τὰ Ἀθεναίο*[*ν*, *δ*]*ẹμευσά*[*ντον τὰ χρέματα αὐτô, hοι δὲ πέντε hοι ἂν ἄ*|*ρ*]*χοσι λαβόντες ἀποδόντ*[*ον τοῖς*] *ἐν τ*[*έλει*] Oliver. The restoration in line 51 hardly fits the sense, since we have just been told that the dikasts will decide the sentence. Furthermore, the use of the aorist in [δ]*ẹμευσά*[*ντον*] is not appropriate to a continuation of the general regulations, yet the restoration of the aorist is certainly right; the new fragment shows that only one letter, which can be no other than delta, is lost at the beginning of the verb

judgments until the reforms of Ephialtes removed such prerogatives. We do not know that Ephialtes did this.

and so nothing but an aorist imperative or infinitive is possible. Oliver's supplement in line 52 is made suspect by the phrase [*hοι* δὲ πέντε *hοι* ἂν ἄρ]χοσι, which implies a revolving board and therefore recurrent problems (*i.e.*, we expect present tenses). Moreover, there must be a stop after λαβόντες. A re-examination of the stone shows that, in line 53, the preserved epsilon on fragment *d* is crowded to the right and so must be preceded by the aspirate. We are thus confronted by ἀποδοντ[. . . . *h*]εντ̣; the lacuna is of four letters. To complete ἀποδόντ[ον] is automatic; [*h*]έντ̣[ινα] is a virtual certainty. We are left with two *stoichoi* and the restoration of [δέ] can scarcely be avoided. So we have someone confiscating something (feminine singular) and then giving it back. Logically, the property confiscated should be that of Milesians already condemned or exiled by previous Athenian decrees, and it should be handed over to returning exiles, those who had remained loyal to Athens. Indeed, the lines may be restored to produce this sense: [τôν δὲ ἐκβεβλεμένον κατὰ τὰ | φ]σεφίσματα τὰ Ἀθεναίο[ν δ]ε̣μευσά[ντον τὲν ὀσίαν *hοι* Μιλέσιοι, *hοπόσες* ἂν τ|ύ]χοσι λαβόντες· ἀποδόντ[ον δὲ *h*]έντ̣[ινα ἂν λάβοσι τοῖς κατελθôσι]. The objection to this interpretation is that the interval between the exile of the rebels and the confiscation of their property is rather long, for these Regulations cannot have been voted immediately after recovery of the city by the Athenians. Another possibility is that, in order to facilitate the return of the loyalists' property, it is to be confiscated by the state from whoever have it and redistributed; then κατερχομένον must replace ἐκβεβλεμένον and τôι ποτε σχόντι the last phrase. If the clause with [τύ]χοσι is correctly restored and if ἀποδίδωμι carries its literal sense, this is the more attractive version: the Milesians will give back to the loyalists ([τôν κατερχομένον]) whatever of their original property they (the present government) may acquire by confiscation. Ὀυσία is unattested in fifth-century inscriptions (cf. χρέματα in lines 28 and 60), but [*h*]έντ̣[ινα] requires a feminine antecedent. Perhaps the choice of noun is governed by the fact that gold and silver are not included here; they appear in the next sentence.

Lines 53–54: [ἀργυ|ρ]ίο Oliver; [χρυ|σ]ίο West; [χρυ]|σ̣ίο BM; the lowest hasta and part of the middle of sigma survive. τι[μέν] Oliver; τιμ[έν] BM; most of mu is on the stone. Of the next letter the stone apparently reveals a low curving stroke; but τιμο[---] cannot be intelligibly restored and we suspect that we have the bottom of an epsilon, freakishly mutilated by the break. We offer an illustration of what we understand the meaning to be: [τô δὲ χρυ]|σ̣ίο hε πόλις ἀποδότο τὲν τιμ[ὲν καὶ τô ἀργυρίο hοπόσα hεκάστοι πρότερον ἐ͂ν]. Miletos is making retribution for the losses in gold and silver suffered by the loyalists. The polis, here and below, means Miletos (*pace* Oliver, p. 196); no such general term would be applied to Athens but, rather, specific officials would be named.

Lines 55–57: πο[ιε͂ν] West. ἐσφορᾶ[ς] Oliver. [κ]|ατεδικάσαντο West. ἀλλέλον hοι οἴκοι οἰ[κôντες (?)] Oliver. The occurrence of *epigraphai* and *eisphora* in consecutive lines has been thought of in terms of the Athenian tax. Mattingly has used the passage as an argument for a date after 427 (*Class. Quart.*, N.S. XVI [1966], p. 190; *A.S.&I.*, p. 208), and Oliver (p. 198) suggested that its imposition by the Athenians may have contributed to Miletos' revolt. But the context, in which it is both preceded and followed by arrangements for retribution, demands that the tax be understood as one that had been imposed by the revolutionary government in Miletos in a harsh and arbitrary manner and in some way used against the exiles. The question of money collected by suit as taxes would naturally have to be differentiated from property confiscated. When the problem was raised, the *syngrapheis* first prohibited assessments of this type in the future. Line 55, which according to Oliver (p. 198) bans all assessments, is most likely merely restrictive; a possible reading is μὲ πο[ιε͂ν παρὰ τὸς πατρίος νόμος]. Then they turned their attention to the law-suits through which the "unjust" tax had been enforced, and we can assume only that they nullified them. It seems clear from line 57, where Oliver's restoration is reasonable, that suits against Milesians who did not leave the city are involved; and surely those against the exiles are included. The required sense may be obtained by the following text: [τὰς δὲ δίκας τὰ|]ς περὶ τôν χρεμάτον τε̂ς ἐσφορᾶ[ς κατὰ τôν φυγάδον ἀκυρίος ε̂ναι καὶ hὰς κ|]ατεδικάσαντο ἀλλέλον hοι οἴκοι οἰ[κôντες]. These suits were not brought by the government but by Milesians who won judgments against one another; it looks as though the Milesians were familiar with what the Athenians called *antidosis*.

Lines 57–61: These lines must continue the disposition of trials about the *eisphora*, since they contain another provision for restitution. The surviving elements of line 58 make reconstruction a formidable task. The word HEXON demands interpretation. In *I.G.*, I², 280, line 75, *hέχον* is a neuter participle, which has no place in our context, especially if the object is [τ]ὲμ πόλιν. Conceivably, one might take the form as the nominative singular masculine of the present participle and cite *hέχοντα* in *I.G.*, I², 374, lines 161 and 176–77. But the mason, or scribe, of the latter was an ancient cockney, who inserted parasitic aspirates lavishly (*e.g.*, *hοικôν*, *hάνδρα*, *hεπί*; see especially *hες ἅς* = ἐς ἅς in line 191); and, again, a nominative singular is out of place. We therefore take HEXON as *hε̂χον*, third person plural of the imperfect tense (for a similar example of ε = ει see προερεμένο[ι]ς in line 38). The expression τὲν πόλιν ἔχειν could mean (1) to occupy the akropolis; (2) to inhabit the city; (3) to possess citizenship (cf. Demosthenes, 21, 106). Here, we believe, we have (2), which of course overlaps (3). In line 58 we find a reference to an alternative, "any other fine." The adjective in line 59 requires a preceding neuter plural, which must be sought in line 57 or 58. This must have some association with ζεμία[ι]. The verb *hε̂χον* is clearly subordinate (the main verb is ε̂ναι in line 59) and its subject belongs in line 57. It is likely that this subject is those loyal Milesians who later went into exile; the sense then is that what the exiles were forced to pay as taxes or were fined while they were still in the city, [*hότε τ*]*ὲμ πόλιν hε̂χον*, is to be returned, as well as (ἒ) what was taken from them under other conditions (*ἄλλει τινί*).

Whatever the exact meaning of these lines, their general purpose is clear: they define what is to be restored to people who have suffered illegal exactions. For with line 59 we are back on firm ground: the first word is undoubtedly [*ἀν*]*απόμπιμα* and the line must have continued with something like *παρὰ τ*[*ὸς πατρίος νόμος*]. Line 60 gives the details of the repayment. On the analogy of line 54, we do not expect officials to be designated here, and lines 59–60 might well have contained [*καὶ τὲμ πόλιν αὐτô*|*ι ἀπ*]*ọδ̣ôναι*. The distinction between *χρέματα* and *ἀργύριον* that follows is strange and implies that there is some special source of repayment other than the Milesian treasury, which can pay only *ἀργύριον*. The reference in line 61 to the Athenian archon may indicate that this source is provided as a result of Athenian decrees passed in this archonship; this is more likely than that the archon-date is part of a deadline for restitution. On the basis of the above argument we propose: [*hὰ δὲ ἀπέτεισαν hοι φυγάδες hότε* | *τ*]*ὲμ πόλιν hε̂χον ἒ ἄλλει τινὶ ζεμία*[*ι hύστερον ἐζεμιόθεσαν, τὰ τιμέματα* | *ἀν*]*απόμπιμα ε̂ναι τôι ὀφλόντι παρὰ τ*[*ὸς πατρίος νόμος καὶ τὲμ πόλιν αὐτô*|*ι ἀπ*]*ọδ̣ôναι ἒ χρέματα ἒ ἀργύριον ἀπὸ* [*τôν δεδεμευμένον κατὰ τὰ ἐφσεφισμ*|*ένα τὰ*] *ἐπ' Εὐθύνο ἄρχοντος*. "What the fugitives paid when they were living in the city or whatever they paid in fines under any other liability, these assessments are to be returned to him who has contrary to the ancestral laws been condemned to pay and the city is to restore to him either goods or cash from the confiscations carried out according to what has been voted in the archonship of Euthynos." We are aware that the syntax is awkward; we do not think it impossible.

Lines 61–62: In all probability these lines contain provisions for the enforcement of what has just preceded. Restoration is made especially difficult by the crowding in 62, where the thirty extant letters occupy twenty-two spaces. Where the crowding began and ended we cannot say; the *vacat* in line 63 might suggest that it stopped there, but in fact this is indecisive since there is a similar *vacat* in line 64 after the regular pattern has apparently been restored. All we can suggest is that the necessity for revision of the original text caused the compression. The five Athenian commissioners are to enforce something. The first preserved letter in line 62, read as iota by Oliver, is nu; the last letter is also nu. The sense, we conjecture, would be satisfied by *hòς δ' ἄμ μὲ [τούτοις πείθεται, αὐτὸν ἀναγκασάν|τον ἀποδõ]ναι*. In the second half of line 62 we are tempted to restore ἐχσεν[εγκόντον γραφὲν περὶ αὐτõ ἐς---]; for a similar use of the verb to describe the action of a board or Council see *I.G.*, I², 76, line 61: *hε δὲ βολὲ ἐς τὸν δε̃μον ἐχσενενκέτο ἐπάναγκες*, where emphasis is on referral *from* the Boule; cf. *A.T.L.*, II, A9, lines 33–34, and *I.G.*, I², 110, lines 37–38 (restored).

Line 62: ἐχσέ[στο (?)] Oliver.

Line 63:]φανον Oliver. Ἀθένε[σι] Oliver. There is an indisputable *vacat* in the *stoichos* before phi; preceding it, at the break, is the upper right tip of a slanting stroke that might be part of sigma, kappa, chi, or upsilon; the word might have been [ἐ]κᵛφανõν or the *vacat* may represent a letter that was not cut. The subject-matter seems not to have changed.

Line 64: Again, we meet an inexplicable uninscribed space. The extant letters bring to mind ἐναντία τοι̃ς Ἀθεναίον σ[υμμάχοις]; for the absent chi cf. line 6. But we do not understand the context.

Lines 65–72: In line 71 there is reference to an oath to be administered by Athenians. The preceding lines are so fragmentary that we cannot identify the beginning of this section. The text of the oath is not given in full, as it is in the decrees dealing with Erythrai, Chalkis, Kolophon, and Samos; it has probably been stipulated in a previous decree. It is possible that lines 65–69 shield provisions for an exchange of oaths between Athenian and Milesian officials (*hοι* πρυτάνες *hοι* Μιλεσ[ίον] in line 65, [*h*]εκάτεροι in line 66, τὸν *h*[όρκον?] in line 67, [*h*]οι μὲν Ἀθε[ναῖοι] in line 68, [ἐ]χσορκ̣[---] in line 69) before provisions for the oaths of the other Milesians [*h*]οι δὲ ἅ[λλοι Μι]λέσι̣[οι], line 70; note μέν and δέ).

Line 65: Μιλεσ[ίον] Oliver. For the Milesian *prytaneis* and the differences between them and the Athenian officials of the same name see Meiggs, *J.H.S.*, LXIII (1943), p. 27, and Barron, *J.H.S.*, LXXXII (1962), pp. 4–5.

Line 66: [*h*]εκάτεροι Oliver; but the crowded epsilon shows that the *daseia* has been inserted.

Line 67: Perhaps τὸν *h*[όρκον].

Line 68: [*h*]οι μὲν Ἀθε[ναῖοι] Oliver.

Line 69: [ἐ]χσόρι[στοι] West. Although some form of ἐξορίζω is of course possible, the upright read as iota is to the left of its *stoichos* and is better interpreted, epigraphically, as kappa; but the lower arm should be visible and is not.

Line 70: [*h*]οι δὲ ἅ[λλοι Μιλ]έσι[οι] Kirchhoff.

Line 71: [*h*]ορκό[ντον δ]ὲ *hοι* πέ[ντε] Kirchhoff; [ἐχσ]ορκό[ντον] is also possible.

Lines 71–72: The lacuna in line 72 before]ν ἄν almost certainly holds [ν πρί]ν. For]εοντο[ν] no uncontracted form is relevant. We therefore assume that we have the imperative of ἐάω. The sense demands that the Five administer the oaths and allow or not allow something before someone swears. We note *hοι* ἄλλοι Μιλέσιοι in line 70 and we envisage a clause along the following lines: [ἐχσ]ορκό[ντον δ]ὲ *hοι* πέν̣[τε μετὰ τôν *h*ορκοτôν μεδὲ ὀμόσαι τὸς ἄλλο|ς Μιλεσίος] ἐόντο[ν πρὶ]ν ἂν ὀμόσε[ι *h*έκαστος τôν πρυτάνεον].

Lines 72–74: [---]ς ὄντο[ς κα]λέτο (?) *h*ὸς ἂν χ [ρ]ε̂ι· *h*ε [---] Kirchhoff; σ[χ]ε̂ι̣ Oliver; [ν Μι]λέτο *h*ὸς ἂν σχε̂ι *h*έ[καστος?] West. ἐπιμελ[ό]σθον *h*όπος ἂν ἄριστ[α] Koumanoudes. The sigma of σ[χ]ε̣̂ι̣ is certain. The letter before]λετο cannot be alpha, of which the lower right hasta would show on the stone. In line 72 there must be another complete change of subject. This section, which continues to line 77, defines the powers of the five Athenian *archontes*. It is tempting to see in line 73 a reference to Miletos and to reconstruct somewhat as follows: [*hοι* δὲ πέντε α|ὐτοκράτορε]ς ὄντο[ν Μι]λέτο *hος* ἂν σ[χ]ε̣ῖ̣ *hε* [πόλις – | —– καὶ] ἐπιμελ[ό]σθον *hόπος* ἂν ἄριστ[α ἄρχεται]. For *hε* [πόλις] we might substitute *hέ*[καστος]; but the lacuna probably hides an expression amounting to law and order. The lines that follow set out the police-powers of the Five, who must therefore have been named before line 74.

Lines 74–77: [Μιλ]εσίον ἒ [τõ]ν φρουρõν κύριοι ὄ[ντ—–] Kirchhoff. μέζονο[ς ἄ]χσιος Koumanoudes. [ἐπιβ(?)]αλόντε[ς *h*]οπόσες ἂν δοκεῖ ἄχσ[ιος ἐ̃ναι] Koumanoudes. [ἐὰν δέ τις ἀπειθε̃ι αὐτο|ῖς ἒ τõν Μιλ]εσίον ἒ [τõ]ν φρουρõν, κύριοι ὄ[ντον αὐτοὶ ζεμιõν μέχρι e.g. δέκα δραχμõ|ν· ἐὰν δέ τις] μ̣έζονο[ς ἄ]χσ[ι]ος ε̣̃ι ζεμίας, Ἀθέ[ναζε καλεσάμενοι αὐτὸν καὶ τὲν ἐπι|βολὲν ἐπιβ]αλόντε[ς *h*]οπόσες ἂν δοκε̃ι ἄχσ[ιος ἐ̃ναι, ἐσαγόντον αὐτὸν ἐς τὸ δικα|στέριον] Oliver, on the basis of Schöll, *Sitzungsb. Ak. München* (1887), p. 19, n. 1. The sense we do not dispute but the restoration is too long, especially because it runs as far as [ἐσφ]ερεσ⟨θ⟩[–––] in line 78, thus forcing the restoration of the unexampled elision [ἐσφ]ερέσ⟨θ⟩[ο δ' ἐ]ς in place of the almost certain infinitive; so we must allow room for a new subject in lines 77–78. In Oliver's version (see his commentary on p. 189) αὐτοῖς, κύριοι, καλεσάμενοι, ἐπιβαλόντες, and ἐσαγόντον all refer to the Five. But the Five are in Miletos and inappropriate as the subject of a verb that requires action (ἐσαγόντον) in Athens. We therefore propose: [ἐὰν δέ τις ἀπειθε̃ι αὐ|τοῖς ἒ τõν Μιλ]εσίον ἒ [τõ]ν φρουρõν κύριοι ὄ[ντον ζεμιõν μέχρι πέντε δραχμ|õν· ἐὰν δέ τις] μέζονο[ς ἄ]χσ[ι]ος ε̣̃ι ζεμίας Ἀθέ[ναζε ἐπὶ δίκεν αὐτὸν προσπεμ|πόντον, ἐπιβ]αλόντε[ς *h*]οπόσες ἂν δοκε̃ι ἄχσ[ιος]. The subject is the Five, who are to send one class of defendant to Athens; the procedure for trials has already been established.

Lines 77–81: ΕΡΕϟΟ lapis; [ἐσφ]έρεσ⟨θ⟩[αι ἐ]ς Kirchhoff; [ἐσφ]ερέσ⟨θ⟩[ο δ' ἐ]ς Oliver (we do not accept the elision, see above). [ἐφσεφ]ίσθαι Hiller. εἴτε ἄλλο τι δ[οκε̑ι ἄχσιον ἐ̑ναι εἴτε μέ] *West*. αὐ[τ]οι̑ς, *Μ*[ιλέ]σιοι, σοφρονο̑[σιν], δέον[ται] Koumanoudes. [..... ἐφσεφ]ίσθαι αὐ̣[το]ι̑ς ἔτι εἴτε ἄλλο τι δ[εέσονται διορθο̑σθαι . . . πρεσβεύο]ντες *Μ*[ιλέ]σιοι· ἐὰν δὲ σοφρονο̑σ[ι .... ἔσται αὐτοι̑ς τυχει̑ν hότο ἄ]ν̣ δέοντ[αι] Mattingly, *Historia*, X (1961), p. 176, n. 127. The subject-matter changes again after ἄχσ[ιος] in line 77 and from here to the end of the document restoration and even understanding are made difficult by sudden shifts of context as minor points are cleared up. What is especially perplexing is the perfect infinitive [ἐφσεφ]ίσθαι. In the fourth century ἐψηφίσθαι may be followed by τη̑ι βουλη̑ι or by τω̑ι δήμωι. In the first case it means that a vote has been taken in the Boule that is to be ratified by the *demos* (ἔδοξεν --- τω̑ι δήμωι); *I.G.*, II^2, 110 (lines 9–10), 152 (lines 12–13). In the second case it means that the *demos* is invited to vote, *i.e.*, let the *demos* vote (the action is in fact still to be taken), and the vote of ratification is to be indicated by ἔδοξεν --- τω̑ι δήμωι: "this is what the *demos will have voted*," in meaning a future perfect. It might be taken as the equivalent of a common imperative. For this usage see *I.G.*, II^2, 43 (line 15), 114 (line 6), 116 (line 9). In each case the infinitive is part of the προβούλευμα; the procedural language differs, the procedure itself does not. This form of expression is not found in the fifth century nor is [ἐφσεφ]ίσθαι αὐ̣[το]ι̑ς a true parallel. Who are αὐ̣[το]ι̑ς? The το̑[ν---] of line 78? Does the verb mean, in effect, that something will have been voted by someone, or that something is to be voted, or that someone (the Boule?) has already (ἔτι) voted? What does ἔτι mean? Is εἴτε preceded or followed by its twin (εἴτε or ε̑ μέ)? What is the transition to the nominative *Μ*[ιλέ]σιοι, which requires a verb? Which Milesians? We set out, in general terms, what we have in mind. Something (perhaps the regulations drawn up by the *syngrapheis*: [hὰ δὲ hοι χσυγγραφε̑ς χσυνέγραφσαν]) is to be introduced into the *demos* by a committee (perhaps the prytaneis: το̑[ν πρυτάνεον]). Some body (αὐ̣[το]ι̑ς, the prytaneis of line 78? They should be members of the Boule but we hesitate to restore an unparalleled usage, *τô[ν βολευτôν]*, in line 78) is invited to vote (on what has already, *ἔτι*, been presented? Or, [*εἴτε*]-- *εἴτε*, on an addition or change, *ἄλλο τι*?). Or, *ἔτι* looks back and *εἴτε* looks forward to the possibility of something else (*εἴτε ἄλλο τι*) requiring a vote? In some way a group of Milesians (perhaps the loyalists who have been in exile, [*hoι κατελθ*]*όντες*; perhaps rebels now in exile, [*hoι φεύγ*]*οντες*) are involved ([*περὶ hôν δέονται hoι*---]*οντες Μ*[*ιλέ*]*σιοι*?). Mattingly's [*πρεσβεύο*]*ντες Μ*[*ιλέ*]*σιοι* seems to us an abnormal usage. The Greek might appear like this: *δ*[*οκεῖ εἴτε μὲ περὶ hôν δέοντα|ι hoι κατελθ*]*όντες* or *δ*[*οκεῖ αὐτοῖς ἒ μὲ περὶ hôν δέο|νται h͜oι φεύγ*]*οντες*. Between *σοφρονο*[---] and [*π*]*ερὶ δὲ Ἀρνασô* we scarcely have room to introduce a new subject along with the necessary apodosis. Therefore *σοφρονο*[---] must be related to the preceding *Μ*[*ιλέ*]*σιοι*. If the Milesians are those already in the city, the protasis supposes their continued good behavior and the sense could be expressed in this way: *ἐὰν δὲ σοφρονô*[*ντες διατελôσι αὐτοί, τυγχα|νόντον hôν ἄ*]*ṿ δέοντ*[*αι*]. If, on the other hand, these Milesians are rebels who are still negotiating, then we should expect no commitment and the sense could be expressed as follows: *ἐὰν δὲ σοφρονô*[*σιν αὐτοί, βουλεύσεται h͜o δêμ|ος περὶ hôν ἄ*]*ṿ δέοντ*[*αι*].

Lines 81–83: [*π*]*ερὶ δὲ Ἀρνασô hε βο*[*λέ*] Koumanoudes; *βο*[*λὲ σκεφσαμένε γνομὲν* (*sic*) *ἐχσενεγκάτο*] Mattingly. *ἄρχοντ*[*αι*] Koumanoudes. [*h*]*ε βο*[*λὲ τὲς φ*]*υλακὲς* Koumanoudes; [*h*]*ε βο*λ̣-[*ὲ ἒ hoι φ*]*ύλακες* Hiller; [*ἐπιμελέσθο δὲ h*]*ε* Lewis, *B.S.A.*, XLIX (1954), p. 24. For Arnasos we can find no other evidence; it must have been a place whose relationship with Miletos remained unsettled. Lewis has pointed out that here, as elsewhere in inscriptions, *φυλακή* must be abstract, not a reference to a garrison. We take it that the Council is to produce a recommendation concerning Arnasos, about which the Milesians have asked a question. In the meantime provisions are made for its government and defense. The sense of our conception could be rendered by: [*π*]*ερὶ δὲ Ἀρνασô hε βο*[*λὲ γνόμεν ἐχσενεγκάτο· hoι* δὲ | πέντε αὐτο]κρ[άτορες ὄν]τον hόπος ἂν ἄρχοντ[αι hοι νῦν ἐκεῖ οἰκôντες· ἐπι|μελέσθο δὲ h]ε βολ[ὲ τε̂ς φ]υλακε̂ς.

Lines 83–84: φσεφ[ισμάτον] Koumanoudes; φσεφ[ισμάτον] *vel* φσεφ[ισθέντον] Kirchhoff; τôν δ' ἐφσεφ[ισμένον] Oliver (but see p. 46, above, on the elision). ἐπιτ[ελε̂]ται Oliver. αὐτοκρά-[τορ] Koumanoudes; αὐτοκράτ[ορ ἔστο] Hiller. These lines obviously give to the Boule the authority to consummate decisions already made.

Lines 84–85: [ἀποσ]τελάντο[ν] Koumanoudes. [δύο] Kirchhoff; [τό] Oliver; Kirchhoff's [δύο] is too long by one letter. The use of the definite article with guard-ships reveals a reference back to arrangements made in lines 8–15. Most likely the generals are responsible and we suggest: [hοι δὲ στρατεγοὶ δέκα | hεμερôν (or αὐτίκα μάλα) ἀποσ]τελάντο[ν τὸ] φρορίδε καὶ τὸς ἄ[λλος φρουρός].

Line 86: [Εὐθ]ύνο Koumanoudes. We can make no sense of what is preserved. The sentence apparently ended after [Εὐθ]ύνο, since the rest of this line and at least one line below have been erased.

Needless to say, we do not claim literal accuracy for the restorations that we have suggested; in fact, we have in the commentary more than once proposed alternatives. We dare to hope, however, that from line 27 to the end we have recovered the sense of these Regulations. To illustrate our conceptions we offer a restored version. Where we restore a crowded *daseia*, we assume that two letters were cut in one *stoichos*, although in some cases three letters or four might have occupied two *stoichoi* or three, as the extant fragments prove.

[Μι]λεσί̣[οις χσυγ]γρ[αφαί]
[ἔδοχσεν] τε̑ι βολε̑ι κα[ὶ τõι δέμοι, ..6...ὶς ἐπρ]υτάν[ευε, ..±6.. ἐγραμμάτ]
[ευε, .±4.]ορ ἐπεστάτε, [Εὔθυνος ἐ̑ρχε· τάδε hοι χ]συγγρα[φε̑ς χσυνέγραφσαν· τε]
[λε̑ν τὰ ν]ομιζόμενα το[ι̑ς θεοι̑ς, hαιρε̑σθαι δ]ὲ πέντε ἄν[δρας τὸν δε̑μον ἐχς hαπ]
[άντον α]ὐτίκα μάλα ὑ̣[πὲρ πεντέκοντα ἔτε] γεγονότ[ας, ἐχσομοσίαν δὲ μὲ ἐ̑να]
[ι αὐτοι̑ς μ]εδὲ ἀνθ⟨α⟩ί[ρεσιν, τούτος δὲ ἄρ]χεν καὶ συν[........19........]
[..7....]οις προσερ̣[.....13.....]ι μετὰ το α̣ι̣[........20........]
[...8....]ενεσι καὶ τ̣ο[....10....]γος τὸς Μιλ[εσίον ....16.......]
[...7... Μιλ]εσίον τὸ[ς ..7....]ο̣γος ΔΕΚΑΤΟ[.........22.........]
[.....11.....] τριερ̣[...8....] τ̣õν στρατιο[τ]ί̣δ[ον ....19........]
[.........22.........] ὅπλα παρέχεσθαι κ̣[.........21.........]
[.........22.........]ε· ὑπερετε̑ν [δ]ὲ τού[τοις ....18........]
[.........20......... τέ]τταρας ὀβο[λὸ]ς π[.........23.........]
[.........21.........]ον hεκ⟨ά⟩στο [τõ] σόμ̣[ατος ....20.........]
[.......16....... Ἀθέν]α̣ζε τοι̑ς στρ̣[α]τιό[τεσι ....21.........]
[.......17....... Ἀθέ]ναζε hότι δ' ἂ̣[ν] τὸ [..........26..........]
[........19........ h]οπόσα ἂν λάβο[σι ....26..........]
[.........20.........]οντος κ[.]οτ̣[..........29..........]
[.......16....... Ἀθέν]α̣ζε hο[...]μ[...........30...........]
[.........21.........] 'Α̣θ̣έ[ν]εσ[ι ....30..........]
[.........21.........]ι[..]αυτ[...........31...........]
[.....13.....]ο̣ι̣ [.4.. h.]ι δὲ σ[...........34...........]
[.....13.....]ιαν[..5..]ιυΓ[...........34...........]
[....10....] τ̣ριάκον[τα ....39............]
[..6... πρ]εσβευτὲς ἐ̑ ε[............40............]
[..6... μ]εδὲν μέτε ἐνδε[...........38........... τ]
[õν χσυ]μμάχον hότι ἂμ μὲ Ἀθε[ναίοις δοκε̑ι ἀγαθόν· hόστις δ' ἂν τοῦτο ποιε̑ι ἄτ]
[ιμο]ς ἔ̣στο καὶ τὰ χρέματα α[ὐτõ δεμόσια ἔστο τε̑ς τε θεõ τὸ ἐπιδέκατον· τὰ]
[ς] δὲ δίκας ἐ̑ναι Μιλεσίοις κα[θάπερ Ἀθεναίοις καὶ χιλίας ἀπὸ τõ ταλάντο]
δραχμ̱ὰς ἀπὸ τõν ἐπιδεκάτο[ν ἐ̑ναι hιερὰς τõι Ἀπόλλονι τõι ἐν Διδύμοις· τὰ]
δ̣ὲ πρυτανει̑α τιθέντον πρὸς [τὸς ἄρχοντας τὸς Ἀθεναίον τὸς ἐν Μιλέτοι· hα]
[ι δ]ὲ δίκαι Ἀθένεσι ὄντον ἐν τ[ε̑ι ἐλιαίαι ἐν τοι̑ς μεσὶ Γαμελιõνι καὶ Ἀνθεσ]
[τε]ριõνι καὶ 'Ελαφεβολιõνι· h[οι δὲ νομοθέται καθιστάντον χιλίος δικαστ]
[ὰς] νέμαντες καὶ κλερόσαντε[ς αὐτὸς κατὰ φυλάς· τὰς δὲ δίκας ταύτας ἀνακ]
[ριν]όντον δύο τõν ἀρχόντον κ[αὶ hοι ἐπιμελεταὶ hοι τõν δικõν καὶ hο μισθὸς δ]
[ιδό]σθο τοι̑ς δικαστε̑σιν ἐκ τọ̃[ν πρυτανείον· καὶ τοι̑ς ἐκ Μιλέτο πορευομέν]
[οις] π̣αρεχόντον τὸ δικαστ[έριον ἐπάναγκες hοι ἀεὶ ἄρχοντες ἐν τοι̑ς μεσὶ]
[τοι̑ς] προερεμένο̣[ι]ς ἐ̑ εὐθυν[όσθον χιλίασι δραχμε̑σι· hόταν δέ τις πρυταν]
[εἰα π]ρ̣ὸς τὸς ἄρχοντας τὸς Ἀθ[εναίον τίθει ....24..........]

[..5..] Ἀθέναζε τοῖς ἐπιμελετ̣[ε͂σι ......31......]
[..5..]αι καθάπερ πρὸ τô καὶ ἐμ̣[......34......]
[...7...]ς ἐπιμελόσθον hοι πέν[τε ......32......]
[..5.. δι]καστέριον καθίζει κ[......34......]
[...7...] πορευομένοις ἐ͂ναι ε[......34......]
[.4..]ˡ[.. h]οι ἄρχοντες hοι Ἀθενα[ίον ......30......]
[..] τελε͂[σθα]ι̣· τὰς δὲ hυπὲρ hεκατὸ[ν δραχμὰς ἐκκλέτος ἐ͂ναι· ταῦτα δὲ γράφσα]
[ι ἐ]ν στέλει̣ [κα]ὶ τοῖς φσεφίσμασ[ι τοῖς Ἀθεναίον ἀεὶ πείθεσθαι Μιλεσίος κ]
[αὶ] μὲ διαφθεί[ρεν] μεδὲ κακοτεχν[ε͂ν hόπος ἂν λυθε͂ι· ἐὰν δέ τις τούτον τι παρ]
α̣βαίνει, γραφαὶ [ὄ]ντον κατ' αὐτô π[ρὸς τὸς ἐπιμελετὰς εὐθύς· hοι δὲ ἐπιμελε]
ταὶ ἐσαγόντον μ[ὲν αὐ]τὸν {ε} ἐς hένα [τôν ἀρχόντον πέντε hεμερôν· τιμάτο δὲ τὸ]
δ̣ικαστέριον hότι ἂγ χ̣[ρε͂]ι̣ παθε͂ν ἒ ἀ[ποτε͂ισαι· τôν δὲ κατερχομένον κατὰ τὰ]
[φ]σεφίσματα τὰ Ἀθεναίο[ν δ]ε̣μευσά[ντον τὲν ὀσίαν hοι Μιλέσιοι, hοπόσες ἂν τ]
[ύ]χοσι λαβόντες· ἀποδόντ[ον δὲ h]έντ̣[ινα ἂν λάβοσι τôι ποτε σχόντι· τô δὲ χρυ]
σ̣ίο hε πόλις ἀποδότο τὲν τιμ[ὲν καὶ τô ἀργυρίο hοπόσα hεκάστοι πρότερον ἐ͂ν.]
καὶ τὸ λοιπὸν ἐπιγραφὰς μὲ πο[ιε͂ν παρὰ τὸς πατρίος νόμος· τὰς δὲ δίκας τὰ]
ς περὶ τôν χρεμάτον τε͂ς ἐσφορᾶ[ς κατὰ τôν φυγάδον ἀκυρίος ἐ͂ναι καὶ hὰς κ]
α̣τεδικάσαντο ἀλλέλον hοι οἴκοι οἰ̣[κôντες· hὰ δὲ ἀπέτεισαν hοι φυγάδες hότε]
[τ]ὲμ πόλιν hε͂χον ἒ ἄλλει τινὶ ζεμία[ι hύστερον ἐζεμιόθεσαν, τὰ τιμέματα]
[ἀν]απόμπιμα ἐ͂ναι τôι ὀφλόντι παρὰ τ[ὸς πατρίος νόμος καὶ τὲμ πόλιν αὐτô]
[ι ἀπ]ο̣δ̣ôναι ἒ χρέματα ἒ ἀργύριον ἀπὸ [τôν δεδεμευμένον κατὰ τὰ ἐφσεφισμ]
[ένα τὰ] ἐπ' Εὐθύνο ἄρχοντος· hὸς δ' ἂμ μὲ [τούτοις πείθεται, αὐτὸν ἀναγκασάν]
[τον ἀποδô]ναι hοι πέντε hοι ἄρχοντες καὶ ἐχσεν[εγκόντον γραφὲν περὶ αὐτô ἐς ––]
[...8....]κ̣^{v}φανον δίκαι ὄντον Ἀθένε[σι ......26......]
[....10....]^{v}ἐναντία τοῖς Ἀθεναίον σ[υμμάχοις ......19......]
[.....12.....] hοι πρυτάνες hοι Μιλεσ[ίον ......24......]
[......15...... h]εκάτεροι τὲμ πόλιν [......27......]
[...7...]ο̣[....11....] Μ̣ιλεσίον τον h[......27......]
[..6...]εσχο̣[.....11..... h]οι μὲν Ἀθε[ναῖοι ......22......]
[..5.. ἐ]χσορκ̣[...8....]ε[..5..]ˡ[..]πει̣[......27......]
[...7... h]οι δὲ ἄ[λλοι Μι]λέσι̣[οι ......34......]
[....9....]ορκό[ντον δ]ὲ hοι πέν̣[τε μετὰ τôν hορκοτôν μεδὲ ὀμόσαι τὸς ἄλλο]
[ς Μιλεσίος] ἐόντο[ν πρὶ]ν ἂν ὀμόσε[ι hέκαστος τôν πρυτάνεον· hοι δὲ πέντε α]
[ὐτοκράτορε]ς ὄντο[ν Μι]λέτο hος ἂν σ[χ]ε͂ι̣ hε [πόλις ......20......]
[...7... καὶ] ἐπιμελ[ό]σθον hόπος ἂν ἄριστ[α ἄρχεται· ἐὰν δέ τις ἀπειθε͂ι αὐ]
[τοῖς ἒ τôν Μιλ]εσίον ἒ [τô]ν φρουρôν κύριοι ὄ[ντον ζεμιôν μέχρι πέντε δραχμ]
[ôν· ἐὰν δέ τις] μέζονο[ς ἄ]χσ[ι]ος ε͂ι ζεμίας Ἀθέ[ναζε ἐπὶ δίκεν αὐτὸν προσπεμ]
[πόντον, ἐπιβ]αλόντε[ς h]οπόσες ἂν δοκε͂ι ἄχσιος· hὰ δὲ hοι χσυνγραφε͂ς χσυν]
[έγραφσαν ἐσφ]έρεσ⟨θ⟩[αι ἐ]ς τὸν δε͂μον hυπὸ τô[ν πρυτάνεον ......14......]
[..5.. ἐφσεφ]ίσθαι αὐ̣[το]ῖς ἔτι εἴτε ἄλλο τι δ[οκε͂ι εἴτε μὲ περὶ hôν δέοντα]
[ι hοι κατελθ]όντες Μ[ιλέ]σιοι· ἐὰν δὲ σοφρονô[ντες διατελôσι αὐτοί, τυγχα]
[νόντον hôν ἂ]ν̣ δέοντ[αι· π]ερὶ δὲ Ἀρνασô hε βο[λὲ γνόμεν ἐχσενεγκάτο· hοι δὲ]

[πέντε αὐτο]κρ[άτορες ὄν]τον hόπος ἂν ἄρχοντ[αι hοι νῦν ἐκεῖ οἰκôντες· ἐπι]
[μελέσθο δὲ h]ε βολ[ὲ τε̂ς φ]υλακε̂ς· τôν δὲ φσεφ[ισ..........22..........]
[....8...ος] ἂν ἐπιτ[ελε̂]ται hε βολὲ αὐτοκράτ[ορ ἔστο· hοι δὲ στρατεγοὶ δέκα]
[hεμερôν ἀποσ]τελάντο[ν τὸ] φρορίδε καὶ τὸς ἄ[λλος φρουρὸς ......13......]
[....10....]σι τον ἐπ' [Εὐθ]ύνο ἄρχοντος ⟦------ *rasura:* traces visible---⟧
⟦------------------------ *rasura* ------------------------⟧

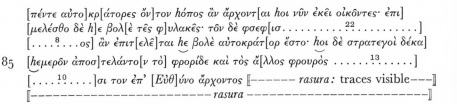

We are now in a position to determine whether this re-examination of the inscription, which, we hope, has increased our knowledge of the settlement with Miletos, contributes to the solution of the problem of its date. Four times has Mattingly attacked the orthodox date, 450/49 B.C., in favor of 426/5, even though he has abandoned some arguments in the face of rebuttal.[24] In a recent statement of his position[25] he is less dogmatic but maintains his dating. We therefore analyze the arguments.

1. "The archon of that year (426/5) was quite certainly Euthynos." Of this there is no doubt; but it does not prove that our text belongs in 426/5. Diodoros names Euthydemos as archon in 426/5 and he gives the same name for 450/49. We know that he (*i.e.*, his source) was wrong for 426/5; he may be equally wrong for 450/49, as Mattingly admits.[26]

2. "*Epimeletai* were elected in 426/5 B.C. with functions similar to those apparently envisaged in *IG*, i², 22+, 42 and 51 f." This argument is without force; it had relevance only when taken with Mattingly's unsupported assumption that the *epimeletai* of D8 were the first officials of this title to be elected.[27] The similarity of function lies merely in the assistance given to archons in trials; see above on lines 34–35. That this should have persisted for a quarter of a century is in no way strange.

[24] For the bibliography see above, n. 3. For rejected arguments see *Class. Quart.*, N.S. XVI (1966), p. 189, n. 3; *A.S.&I.*, p. 221, n. 87.

[25] *A.S.&I.*, pp. 207–209.

[26] The common assumption of an error by Diodoros depends basically upon the dating of this decree to mid-century. The name of the archon, then, is in the first instance irrelevant to the problem of the decree's date. We note that Meritt, Wade-Gery, and McGregor, *A.T.L.*, II, p. 61, assume the same error in the papyrus-decree, D13.

[27] *Historia*, X (1961), p. 177; but see Meritt and Wade-Gery, *J.H.S.*, LXXXIII (1963), p. 102, and the commentary on lines 34–35 above.

3. "The mention of *ἐπιγραφαί* and *χρημάτων εἰσφορά* in lines 57 f. recalls the first Athenian *eisphora* of the war in 428/7 B.C. and the establishment of the *φόρου ἐκλογεῖς* in allied cities two years later." The text, we believe, confirms that neither of these alleged connections with the 'twenties and Athens is tenable; see above on lines 55–57. Apart from our restorations, which may not be literally accurate, the extant words show that the significant expressions are part of a passage concerning the restoration of money and property in Miletos.[28]

4. "Lines 10–20 seem to arrange for provision of troops by Miletos for service in Greece and, while this would be surprising in 450/49 B.C. (during the Five Years' Truce), we know from Thucydides that Milesian hoplites fought in Nikias' Corinthian campaign of late summer 425 B.C." These lines are so fragmentary that no argument can be based upon them, although our view is that the reference is to the sending of the new board to Miletos and reorganization of the garrison; see the commentary on lines 10–23 and 84–85.

These are Mattingly's principal supports, two of which (2 and 3), without doubt, are eliminated by a proper understanding of the text; one (4) never had any real basis and the other (1) remains irrelevant. Mattingly adds another argument, which we do not rank with the listed four since even he admits that he "would not wish to push this argument very far." It rests upon the mention of *phrourides* and *stratiotides* (lines 85 and 10) and upon the assumption that these terms "had not been long established as technical jargon when Thucydides left Athens for exile in 424 B.C." because the historian uses *stratiotides* and *hoplitagogoi* interchangeably. We dismiss this point as trivial, especially since *hoplitagogoi* appear nowhere in inscriptions and, as Mattingly himself confesses, the "use of triremes for blockade and troop-carrying . . . was obviously familiar to the Athenians long before 431 B.C."

[28] See especially *ἀποδόντ[ον]*, line 53; *ἀποδότο*, 54; *[ἀν]απόμπιμα*, 59; *[ἀπ]ọδ̣ο̂ναι*, 60.

Mattingly then confronts, in a cursory manner, the two chief objections to his dating. The first is Thucydides' silence about trouble in Miletos in the 420s; this difficulty he tries to circumvent by the supposition that the decree is the result of an "abortive attempt at revolt . . . swiftly crushed by a routine operation involving only a few ships." He also appeals to the imagined silence of Thucydides about "intervention in 424/3 B.C., which crushed incipient disloyalty at Chalkis and Eretria"; but this heresy depends largely on his untenable dating of *I.G.*, I², 39, to that year.[29] The second objection is that this legislation seems to have "left an oligarchic government in power—a hardly credible proceeding after *stasis* in the Archidamian War." Mattingly's answer is as follows: "The decree certainly did not in itself establish democracy, but I am prepared to believe that it was designed to create conditions in which a democratic system could be evolved." We do not really understand Mattingly's view of what had happened at Miletos. He accepts (pp. 207–208) Barron's reconstruction of internal events there, including the presence of democratic government after 443. Yet, if democratic government did persist until 426/5, when it was threatened by an "abortive attempt at revolt," there was hardly need for a commission to create conditions that could lead to its evolution.

The two arguments, which are not satisfactorily answered by Mattingly, are so strengthened by comprehension of the decree as a whole as to make the date 450/49 virtually certain. The elimination of the reference to the *prosetairoi* in line 7, which might seem to weaken the second argument, is more than offset by the realization that the word πόλις (lines 54 and 66) means Miletos, a usage that is not consonant with the existence of democratic government. Furthermore, the degree of Athens' detailed

[29] *J.H.S.*, LXXXI (1961), pp. 124–32. Mattingly has now adopted 424/3 as a firm date; see *A.S.&I.*, p. 211: "Slanting lambdas are found in the Chalkis Decree of 424/3 B.C." It is true that no refutation of the original case has appeared; but it seems to us so weak as scarcely to merit one.

concern for Milesian judicial procedure implies that there were no democratic courts there that she could trust at the time.[30]

It is, however, the argument from Thucydides' silence that gains most force from what our new understanding of the text tells us of the situation that preceded its passage. The troubles must have been widespread and serious to demand the special court for the Milesian offenders and such drastic powers for the Athenian commission (see lines 28–51 with commentary). The detail and space devoted to the restoration of money and property to those who can be none other than returned exiles show that an anti-Athenian government must have been in control for some time (see lines 51–62 with commentary).

It is now profitable to review the evidence of the quota-lists.[31] We tabulate the record as published in *A.T.L.*, I and II:

List 1, VI, 19–22 (454/3)
Μιλέσιοι
[ἐ]χς *Λέρο:* HHH
[*Μι*]λέσιοι
[ἐκ *Τ*]ειχιόσσε[ς: --]
List 3, II, 28 (452/1)
--- *Μιλέσ*[ιοι]

The authors of *A.T.L.* conclude that, with Miletos in revolt in 454/3, the loyalists in the dependencies Leros and Teichioussa met their obligations, at least in part; that the appearance of *Μιλέσ*[ιοι] in 452/1 represents the return to allegiance. They further suggest (III, p. 255, n. 49) that Latmos, a close associate of Miletos, may also have revolted, in which case the entry *Λάτμιοι* in 2, X, 3 shows that the town had been recovered by the spring of 453/2, the first step in the full assertion by Athens of her hegemony in this area. Mattingly, however, is worried[32] by the long interval, about three years, between the quelling

[30] Cf. *I.G.*, I², 39, lines 71–76, where the Chalkidian courts, under democracy, are given much authority.
[31] See *A.T.L.*, III, pp. 253, 255–56.
[32] *A.S.&I.*, p. 207.

of the revolt and the Regulations. We see no great difficulty; this document is obviously not the first step[33] in the settlement of Milesian affairs (see the commentary on lines 61, 65–72), and a commission appointed to solve specific problems, especially the complicated one of restitution, might well have deliberated for some time.

It is part of the fascination of our studies that additional evidence is ever likely to appear, to confirm or confound the historian's reconstruction. So it is now: a new fragment of List 1, of relevance to Milesian affairs, came to light in the Agora in the excavations of 1971. The piece will be published and discussed thoroughly in an early number of *Hesperia* by B. D. Meritt. It is his belief and ours that the evidence of this new fragment supports the reconstruction that we have advanced of the fate of Miletos in the first assessment-period.

We find ourselves strikingly impressed by the extent to which this decree and the evidence of the quota-lists complement each other. The decree, then, is peculiarly appropriate to a serious revolt in the 'fifties (and Barron's reconstruction[34]) but not at all to an "abortive attempt at revolt" in the 'twenties. This point, we believe, is conclusive in favor of the traditional dating.[35]

It will, no doubt, have been noted that in discussion of the date we have made no mention of letter-forms, which do in fact corroborate the earlier date.[36] Our own approach to Attic decrees of the fifth century has been governed by our hopes of

[33] *A.T.L.*, III, p. 256: "The Athenian decree which brought Miletos back into the Confederacy in 452 has not been preserved. The regulations of D11 are subsequent to the initial reconciliation; they do not contain the oath of allegiance. . . ."

[34] *Op. cit.*, pp. 5–6.

[35] We remind the reader that our argument has been based on those sections of the decree in which the general sense is clear; we do not, of course, depend on the very tentative restorations of lines 72–74. C. W. Fornara, *A.J.P.*, XCII (1971), pp. 473–75, denies that the mention of Euthynos dates the Regulations and places the document shortly after 442. We disagree; we consider that his judgment, expressed with no reference whatever to epigraphic criteria, is hasty.

[36] Meiggs, *J.H.S.*, LXXXVI (1966), 86–98, especially 97.

reaching secure dates through the internal evidence. In the case of the Regulations for Miletos we believe that this can be done and we feel justified in stating that here we have still another decree with the three-barred sigma correctly dated before 445 B.C.

CHAPTER III

The Alliance With Egesta

(Plates VIII–IX)

The stele bearing the Athenian treaty with Egesta has in recent years become notorious.[1] The archon's name, which would of course date the text securely, was engraved in line 3, where, infuriatingly, the stone is so worn that his identity has caused vigorous controversy. We have new readings in line 1 and views about line 3 based upon a careful and prolonged scrutiny of the stone. We present text and commentary.

458/7 B.C. *ΣΤΟΙΧ.* 48

[Χσυμμαχία καὶ hόρ]κ̣ο[ς] Ἀ̣[θ]ε̣ν̣α̣[ίον κα]ὶ Ἐγεσταί[ον]
[ἔδοχσεν τε̑ι βολε̑ι καὶ τ]ο̑ι [δέμοι· ..6...ὶς] ἐπρυτάνευε, [.4..]
[.±4. ἐγραμμάτευε, .±4.]ο[.4.. ἐ]π̣[εστάτε, hά]β̣[ρ]ον ἔ̑ρχε, Ἀρ[..4.]
[... εἶπεν· περὶ Ἐγεστα]ίο[ν τὸ]ν [hό]ρ̣[κον εὐθὺς δ]ο̣̂ν̣α̣ι̣ αὐ̣το[ῖς ..]
[.........20.........]οσα̣[.......16.......]δ[..]ε[..5..]

[1] *I.G.*, I², 19 (EM 6568), to which Raubitschek acutely added lines 1–2 of the smaller fragment published as *I.G.*, I², 20 (EM 6806); *T.A.P.A.*, LXXV (1944), pp. 10–14 (photograph of a squeeze of *I.G.*, I², 20 opposite p. 13). The first publication of the longer piece was by U. Köhler, *Hermes*, II (1867), pp. 16–18, whose text appeared later as *I.G.*, I, 20 (Kirchhoff). Lolling, *Δελτ. Ἀρχ.* (1891), pp. 105–108, re-examined the stone. Woodhead printed a text in *Hesperia*, XVII (1948), pp. 58–60 (photograph on Pl. 24). Mattingly discusses the text and the date, *Historia*, XII (1963), pp. 267–69; *Atti del I Convegno del Centro Internazionale di Studi Numismatici* (1967), *Annali*, XII–XIV, *Supplemento* (1969), pp. 201–21, especially 204–206. Meiggs and Lewis, *G.H.I.*, include the treaty as no. 37 (Tod, *G.H.I.*, I², no. 31). For further bibliography see *S.E.G.*, X, 7; XII, 6; XIV, 1; XXI, 10; XXII, 3; and for photographs see Plates VIII (*I.G.*, I², 19) and IX (*I.G.*, I², 20). We have had available the text prepared by Woodhead for *I.G.*, I³.

[.........21..........]σ[.]ι̣[.....12.....]αι τὸς δι̣[..5..]
[.........19.........]ερ[....]ο[....]ι̣[τ]α̣ [h]ιερὰ [h]όσομπ̣[ε]ρ̣ ε[.]
[........18........ τ]ὸν hό[ρκ]ον̣ ὀ̣[μνύν]α̣[ι· hόπ]ος δ᾽ ἂν ὀμό[σοσ]
[ιν hάπαντες hοι στρατ]εγοὶ ἐπιμελεθέν[τον παρ]αγγ[ε]λ[..5..]
[........18........ τ]ôν hορκοτôν hόπ[ος ..5..]εγ[...7...]
[.....11.....· τὸ δὲ φσέ]φισμα τόδε καὶ τὸν hόρκ]ο[ν] ἀνα[γρ]ά̣[φσα]
[ι ἐστέλει λιθίνει ἐμ π]όλει τὸν γραμματέα τε̂ς βολε̂ς· [hοι δὲ π]
[ολεταὶ ἀπομισθοσάντ]ον· hο[ι] δὲ κολακρέται δό[ν]το[ν τὸ ἀργύρ]
[ιον· καλέσαι δὲ καὶ ἐπ]ὶ χσένια τὲν πρεσβείαν τôν ᾽Ε[γεσταίον]
[ἐς πρυτανεῖον ἐς τὸν] νομιζόμενον χρόνον. *v* Εὔφεμ[ος εἶπε· τὰ]
[μὲν ἄλλα καθάπερ τε̂ι β]ολε̂ι· τὸ δὲ λοιπὸν ἐπειδὰν π̣[ρέσβες ᾽Εγ]
[εσταίον ἀφικνôνται hο κ]ε̂ρυχς προσαγ[έτο ......14......]
[............25.............]ς π[.........21..........]

lacuna

[πρέσβες] ᾽Εγεσταί[ον hοίδε τὸν hόρκον ὄμνυον· .....12.....]
[...7...]ικίνο Ἀπ[...............34................]

vacat

Line 1: [συμμαχία Ἀ]θ[εναίον κα]ὶ ᾽Εγεσταί[ον] Hiller; [φιλία καὶ χσυνμαχία Ἀθεναίον καὶ] ᾽Εγεσταί[ον] Woodhead (1948). There is no doubt about the circular letter interpreted as theta by Hiller (it also appears in *I.G.*, I, 20). It lies slightly to the right of [τ]ôι in the line below (and, to use a more easily legible area, the sigma of [φσέ]φισμα in line 11). The required restoration of line 2, with [τ]ôι as the definite article of the normal introductory formula, and the preservation of the right side of the stone show that each line of the decree proper (the text is *stoichedon*) contained forty-eight letters and that the iota of [τ]ôι is the twenty-first. Enough is extant of the larger and more widely spaced letters of line 1 for us to compute mathematically that the line is of thirty-eight letters and that the circular letter occupies the seventeenth *stoichos*.[2] We therefore restore [χσυμμαχία καὶ hόρ]κ̣ο[ς] Ἀ̣[θ]ε̣ν̣α̣[ίον κα]ὶ ᾽Εγεσταί[ον]. For the association of ξυμμαχία and ὅρκος see *I.G.*, I², 51, lines 1–2; 52, lines 2–4; Thucydides, V, 47, 11 (*I.G.*, I², 86). Of kappa we

[2] The spacing in line 1, admittedly, is not uniform. In line 2 [τ]ôι completes twenty-one *stoichoi*, which are followed by twenty-seven. The circular letter in line 1 is now preceded by sixteen and followed by twenty-one. The proportions match almost exactly.

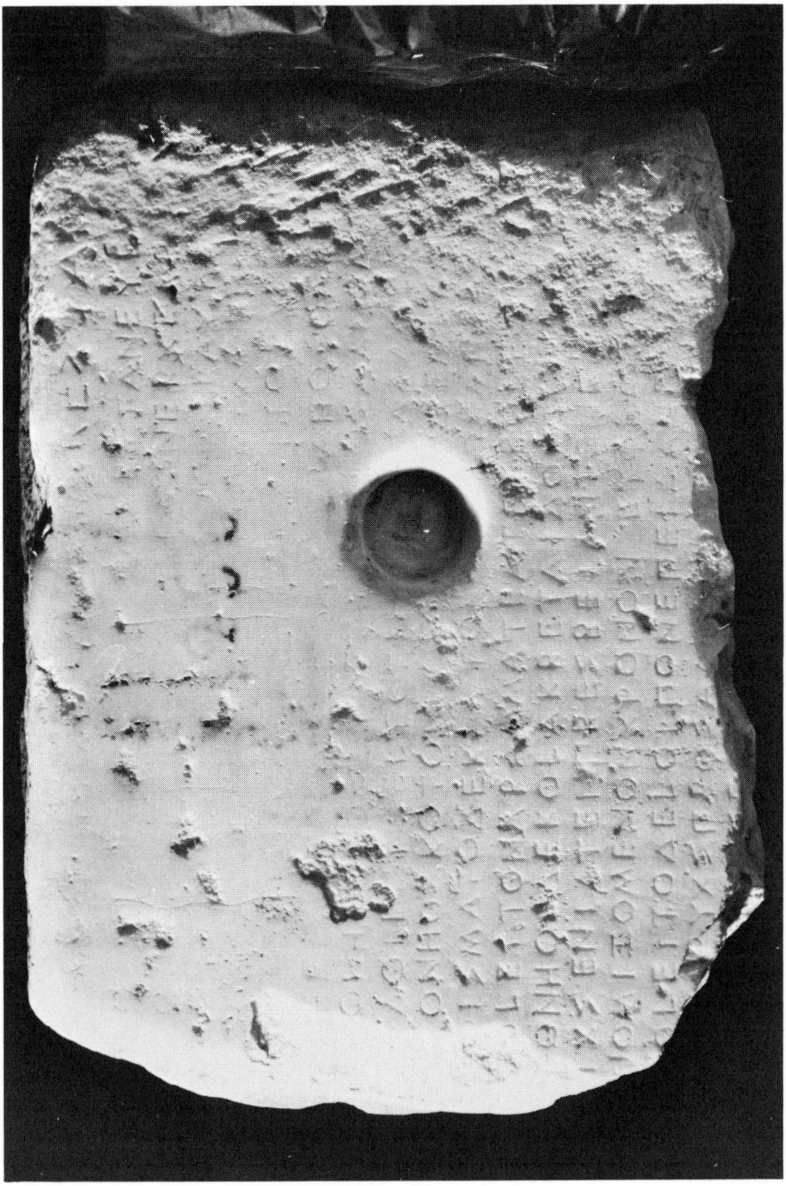

Plate VIII. *I.G.*, I^2, 19, the Treaty with Egesta, upper fragment (*Photograph courtesy of the National Epigraphic Museum*)

Plate IX. *I.G.*, I², 20, the Treaty with Egesta, lower fragment (top two lines) (*Photograph courtesy of the National Epigraphic Museum*)

detect a trace of the vertical and the tip of the lower arm; of alpha the lower tip of the left side; of epsilon the lower tip of the vertical and a suggestion of the lowest horizontal; of nu the lower tips of the two uprights; of alpha the left side; of iota (read by Köhler and Hiller) the lower tip.

Line 2: We read the iota of [τ]ôι and ἐπρυτάνευε, in which no letter requires a dot, in its entirety.

Line 3: --]◌◌N Köhler and Kirchhoff; [Ἀρίστ]ον Lolling; [Ἀρίστ]ον Hiller; [hά]β̣ρ̣ον Raubitschek; [hά]β̣ρ̣ον Woodhead (1948), --] I.ον (1969); [h]ά̣β̣[ρ]ον Klaffenbach (*per epistolas, ectypo usus*, *S.E.G.*, X, 7); [Ἀντ]ι̣φ̣ôν Mattingly; [hάβρ]ον Meiggs and Lewis. There is no doubt about the final omicron and nu of the name; we concentrate on the preceding three letters, beginning with Klaffenbach's reported alpha. There is no trace whatever of cutting on the stone; so far as we know, nothing has been read from the stele in this letter-space.

In May, 1968, Donald R. Laing visited Berlin and was kind enough, at our request, to scrutinize the squeeze in question, which is now in the files of the Academie der Wissenschaft. This is his report: "There are no clear and unquestionable letter-strokes visible on the squeeze in this space. However, I observed a faint but definitely triangular shape on the squeeze that could be the result of the wearing down of an A or Δ, but one cannot exclude other letters as well. I tried to measure this in so far as I could mark its limits and its "apex" seemed to be about .01 m. from the top of the following vertical shaft in the next letter-space. The slanting side approached this shaft toward the base to a point .003 m. away, as far as I could measure. In certain lights I got the impression of a horizontal mark or change in the appearance of this area at the height appropriate to the cross-bar of an alpha but this was very elusive and I could not measure it precisely. This triangular area seemed to me to be a bit crowded laterally with the next letter-stroke in comparison with the rest of the text, and also slightly out of line, that is, it seemed to tip a bit. This remains my general impression. Upon my return to Athens I re-examined the stone itself but in its present condition I could see no traces at the appropriate place that might have produced such an impression on the squeeze." On the basis of Laing's report and the evidence of our own eyes we refrain from reading any letter, however tentatively, in this *stoichos*.[3]

The upright hasta in the next *stoichos*, we believe, is the mark of the chisel.[4] The hook at the top, however, which makes an angle that does not fit a letter and is very light, is a mere scratch. Mattingly asserts[5] that "the vertical stroke indeed is in the exact centre of the letter-space." This is not so. The placement of letters one beneath another on this stele is in fact a little irregular, as anyone can demonstrate with a plumb-line. For example, the thirtieth *stoichoi* in lines 14–16 are occupied respectively by epsilon, rho, and pi. One can see with the naked eye that the vertical hasta of pi is to the left of the vertical hasta of rho, which is to the left of the vertical hasta of epsilon. Our own prolonged and repeated tests convinced us that the vertical in line 3 is neither centered nor at the extreme left; it is more to the left than to the center. Nonetheless, it lies immediately below the vertical stroke of epsilon in the *stoichos* above. In other words it could belong to a letter requiring a left-hand vertical or to one requiring a centered vertical; its position is not conclusive. In the next *stoichos* Köhler read a broken circular letter, which Raubitschek translated into a dotted rho and Mattingly into a dotted phi. We certainly see a number of marks on the stone, which one might well be tempted to transform into the oval of phi. But they do not form a continuous line, the left-hand side is suspiciously flat, and, most significant of all, this roughly oval shape is cut, above and below, by similar scratches; for scratches,

[3] This was also the conclusion of Meritt, *B.C.H.*, LXXXVIII (1964), pp. 413–15, who in note 2 quotes Klaffenbach's words.

[4] Note Laing's apparent acceptance of this "shaft."

[5] *Historia*, XII (1963), p. 269; cf. his note 57: "*IG* i^2, 19 is strictly stoichedon in arrangement."

probably, are what we are discussing. We conclude that they were not made by a chisel and that they are not the relics of any letter. In this *stoichos* nothing can be read and nothing can even be suspected. The optimist can read no more than these pitiful remnants of the archon's name: [---]I[.]*ον*. Even so, we can make progress.

We are seeking an archon whose name ends in omega nu. We shall not, we hope, be considered arbitrary if we restrict the period to the years between the opening of the first Peloponnesian war and the Sicilian expedition.[6] Our candidates are Habron (458/7), Ariston (454/3), Epameinon (429/8), Aristion (421/0), and Antiphon (418/7). Ariston, however, loses his place because the sigma in his name is incompatible with our reading of the stone. For further progress we must turn to letter-forms.

For many years epigraphists were accustomed to assign dates to fifth-century documents on the basis of the shapes of certain crucial letters, such as rho, beta, phi, and especially sigma; it was accepted as orthodox doctrine that the three-barred form of sigma disappeared from official Attic documents about 445 B.C. In 1961 H. B. Mattingly[7] began an assault on these methods of dating that he has maintained ever since. His chief target has been the "law" of the three-barred sigma. So far, one systematic reply has appeared, by R. Meiggs,[8] who made a careful study of the shapes of beta, rho, phi, and sigma in dated inscriptions of the period 460–30 and then applied his results to undated documents. The last dated three-barred sigma was cut in 446, the last dated tailed rho in 438 B.C.[9] Meiggs' conclusion is worth quoting: "The evidence of

[6] We thus exclude Konon (462/1), Apsephion (469/8), Demotion (470/69), and Menon (473/2).

[7] *Historia*, X (1961), pp. 148–88: "Is it really true that three-bar sigma disappears from Attic epigraphy after 445 B.C.?" (p. 149); *J.H.S.*, LXXXI (1961), pp. 124–32; more recently *A.S.& I.* (1966), pp. 193–223.

[8] *J.H.S.*, LXXXVI (1966), pp. 86–98.

[9] *A.T.L.*, II, List 8; *I.G.*, I², 354. It is interesting to note that no tailed rho appears in Meiggs' table (p. 92) of dated documents between 447 B.C. (*A.T.L.*, II, List 7) and 438.

dated inscriptions between 445 and 430 is too consistent to be ignored. Until examples of the early forms of sigma, beta, rho or phi are found in inscriptions securely dated after 445 we should continue to date all inscriptions using any of the early forms except rounded rho with tail before 445." We ourselves spent the year 1967–68 studying the shapes of all letters in the public documents of the fifth century. We have not yet completed our task but all our results so far and all our impressions support what Meiggs wrote in 1966. Michael Walbank, in his two-year examination of Attic proxenies, looked at every public document of the fifth century and he is in complete agreement with us.

In the case of the Treaty with Egesta, the consistent use of the three-barred sigma is sufficient, we think, to restrict us to a date before 445. When, in addition, we find the tailed rho, then the cumulative evidence is close to overwhelming. So we are left with only one archon, Habron, who satisfies the epigraphic requirements: [*hά*]*β̣*[*ρ*]*ον*.

We turn to historical considerations. The argument against [*Ἀντ*]*ι̣φôν*, which on epigraphic grounds may be regarded as superfluous, is strong. In the winter of 416/5 the Egestaians, seeking aid, came to Athens, *τὴν γενομένην ἐπὶ Λάχητος καὶ τοῦ προτέρου πολέμου Λεοντίνων . . . ξυμμαχίαν ἀναμιμνῄσκοντες τοὺς Ἀθηναίους* (Thucydides, VI, 6, 2). Laches had been in command from the summer of 427 (III, 86, 1) to the winter of 426/5 (III, 115). Whatever the precise meaning of the Greek (see the recent notes of Dover in Gomme, Andrewes, and Dover, *Commentary*, IV, p. 221), would the Egestaians, in their emergency, have ignored a treaty made two years earlier, in the archonship of Antiphon, and yet have cited an alliance of a decade ago?

Meiggs and Lewis, *G.H.I.*, p. 81, write: "We have not been able to confirm a curving stroke [*sc.* before omicron], and we still feel doubtful whether the vertical is part of a letter. Of the three dates [*sc.* 458/7, 454/3, 418/17] we would rule out 418–17, because we know of no dated ϟ after 445, and no R after

438–7. . . . It is also unlikely that Thucydides would have failed to mention it in his introduction to the Sicilian expedition, had Egesta exchanged oaths with Athens so recently." Having thus placed the treaty in the 450s, they go one step further: "On broad historical grounds Athens is more likely to have accepted commitments in Sicily in the early fifties, when the war against the Peloponnesians and the Egyptian expedition were running strongly in her favour, than in 454–3 when the Athenian and allied forces in Egypt, if not already overwhelmed, had at least been driven from Memphis and blockaded on Prosopitis. We prefer [*hάβρ*]*ον*."

We print [*hά*]*β̣*[*ρ*]*ον* and so identify the upper part of a left-hand vertical in the twenty-sixth *stoichos* as the pi of ἐπεστάτε. We recognize that not all accept the vertical that we have interpreted as beta. If we were to dismiss beta, then we should be left with [---]*ον*, but we should still insist that the alliance be placed in the fifties; *i.e.*, the archon is [*hάβρ*]*ον* or [*Ἀρίστ*]*ον*. We are attracted by the preference for Habron argued by Meiggs and Lewis but do not find it conclusive.

Lines 3–4: Ἀρ[χέ]δ̣ε|[μος? εἶπε] Hiller, followed by Woodhead (1948); Ἀρ[χί]α̣[ς | εἶπεν] (1969). We have grave doubts about the stroke interpreted as the right-hand diagonal of delta or alpha. It is rough and deep, 0.014 m. in length as opposed to the normal 0.011 m. There is no trace of the chisel in the following *stoichos* and, like Köhler and Kirchhoff, we show no letters after Ἀρ[, the beginning of the orator's name, which probably extended into the next line.

Lines 4–7: The new readings are ours. In the thirty-eighth *stoichos* of line 4 the verticals of nu are visible. The following alpha is merely suggested by the smooth stone. The fortieth letter is not tau; the stroke is to the left and there is no sign of a cross-bar, but iota is possible. The preceding letter might be alpha. There is no diagonal (Hiller) in the forty-fifth *stoichos*. In line 5 the left-hand diagonal survives of the first triangular letter. The second is delta, not alpha (Hiller). In line 7 the thirty-first letter may be epsilon or pi or nu. Woodhead now (1969) proposes, tentatively:

[εἶπεν· περὶ μὲν 'Εγεστα]ίο[ν τὸ]ν [hό]ρ̣[κον εὐθὺς
δ]ôν[α]ι αὐτο[ῖς ἐπ]
[ὶ χσυμμαχίαι τοστρατεγ]ὸς Ἀ̣[θένεσιν· δέχσασθαι] δ'
['Εγ]έ[σται π]
[αρὰ αὐτôν· Ἀθεναίον δὲ ὀμό]σ[α]ι̣ [καὶ τὲμ βολὲν κ]αὶ
τὸς δι̣[καστὰ]
[ς κατὰ ταὐτά· ἐς δὲ καλλι]έρ[εσιν] θ̣[υσιô]ν̣ [τ]ὰ [h]ι̣ερὰ κτλ.

We prefer [. . . εἶπεν· περὶ 'Εγεστα]ίο[ν] because Attic decrees commonly begin without the particle. For the rest, we are made uneasy by the fact that the generals swear the oath at Athens and then the council and the dikasts do likewise, *κατὰ ταὐτά*. Further, lines 5–6, with their vague reference to reception of the oath at Egesta, scarcely suit the specific action of line 19, where the envoys are recorded as having sworn. Lines 5–6, in fact, should tell us that the envoys are to swear. We do not print a restoration in our text but we illustrate our understanding of the sense of the passage, at the same time respecting what little the years have preserved on the stone:

[δ]ο̣̂να̣ι̣ αὐτο[ῖς κα]
[ὶ δέχσασθαι παρ' αὐτôν· ὀμ]όσα̣[ι μὲν 'Εγεσταίον τέν]δ[ε
τ]ὲ[ν νûν π]
[ρεσβείαν· Ἀθεναίον δὲ ὀμό]σ[α]ι̣ [καὶ τὲν βολὲν κ]αὶ τὸς δι̣[καστά]
[ς· καὶ ho βασιλεὺς καλλι]ερ[εσάτ]ο [ἅμεμ]π̣[τ]α̣ [h]ιερὰ
[h]όσομπ̣[ε]ρ̣ 'Ε[γ]
[εσταῖοι ἐπιθυμôνται τ]ὸν hό[ρκ]ον̣ ὀ̣[μνύν]α̣[ι].

The Boule and the *dikastai* swear the oath in the Treaty with Chalkis; *I.G.*, I², 39, 3–4 (*A.T.L.*, II, D17). The same function is performed by the Boule and the *ἔνδημοι ἀρχαί* in Thucydides' text (V, 47, 9) of the Treaty with Argos, Mantineia, and Elis (*I.G.*, I², 86).

Lines 9–11: In line 10 the dotted gamma is an interpretation of a left-hand slanting stroke; but alpha or mu or delta is possible; 'Εγ̣[εσταιο] Woodhead. Nothing is visible before the epsilon. We suggest:

[παρ]αγγ[έ]λ[αντες]
[τοῖς πρυτανεῦσι μετὰ τ]ο̂ν hορκοτο̂ν hόπ[ος ἂν τὸς] 'Εγ̣[εσταίος]
[ἐχσορκόσοσι].

The *prytaneis* administer the oath in Thucydides' text (V, 47, 9) of the Treaty with Argos, Mantineia, and Elis in 420/19 B.C.

Lines 16–17: π̣[ρέσβες ἔλ|θοσιν ἀπ' 'Εγεσταίον hο κ]ε̂ρυχς Woodhead (1948); [*hέκοσιν*] Tod. This restoration, repeated since 1948, is impossible: the lacuna in line 17 before]ερυχς is of twenty letters, not nineteen. The fortieth letter in line 16 is pi or epsilon.

CHAPTER IV

Athens and the Boiotians

(Plates X–XIII)

This document comprises five fragments of Pentelic marble with a faint bluish tinge, of which fragment 1 (= *a*) was published as *I.G.*, I², 68, fragments 4 and 5 (= *c* and *b*) appeared as *I.G.*, I², 69. Fragment 2 was edited by Oliver, *A.J.A.*, XL (1936), pp. 460–61 (= *S.E.G.*, X, 81), and added to the other pieces by Meritt, *Hesperia*, XIV (1945), pp. 105–15 (= *S.E.G.*, X, 81). Michael Walbank identified fragment 3 and effected the join with fragment 2. Bradeen and McGregor joined fragments 2 and 5 to fragment 4. All fragments are now in the Epigraphic Museum, fragments 2–5 set in plaster; for a photograph see Plate X.

Fragment 1, EM 6611. Height 0.21 m. (with the molding of 0.073 m.), width 0.423 m., thickness 0.133 m. Broken on all sides except the top, which is smooth-picked. For the molding, the upper fascia of which was inscribed, see Plate XI.

Fragment 2, EM 12830. Height 0.235 m., width 0.475 m., thickness 0.155 m. Smooth-picked left side and rough-picked back preserved. See Plate X. Meritt gives a photograph of a squeeze, *op. cit.*, p. 107.

Fragment 3, EM 5417 (unpublished). Height 0.081 m., width 0.096 m., thickness 0.071 m. Left side preserved. See Plate X.

Fragment 4, EM 6622. Height 0.275 m., width 0.245 m., thickness 0.144 m. Rough-picked back preserved. See Plate XII.

Fragment 5, EM 6621. Height 0.277 m., width 0.285 m., thickness 0.095 m. Broken on all sides. See Plate XIII.

The lettering is Attic, non-*stoichedon*, and untidily cut. The *daseia* is not used; sigma is four-barred. For the letter-forms, which vary (especially lambda, nu, sigma, rho), see Plates X–XIII. The vertical spacing increases from top to bottom, *ca* 0.017 m. to *ca* 0.019 m. Horizontally, there is much irregularity.

The line of fracture at the bottom of fragment 1 is so similar to that at the top of fragment 2 that we sought a join. But projections on fragments 2 and 4 prove that physical union is out of the question. We have therefore placed the two fragments as close to one another as may be, thus making the top line of 2, where we read two vertical strokes, line 8 of fragment 1. The interval between the two fragments may in fact be slightly larger; it cannot be smaller. Between line 8 (fragment 1) and line 13 (fragment 4) the lacuna is of four lines at least.

The initial lacuna in line 4 is of twenty-two letters, which governs, approximately, its position laterally. The distance from the edge of the stone in line 13 to the twenty-third letter, the gamma of ἐσεγôντ̣[αι], is 0.286 m. We therefore place fragment 1 in such a way that the initial preserved epsilon of line 4 is 0.286 m. from the left edge. There is of course a margin of error in such computations because the text is not *stoichedon*.

It is impossible to compute precisely the original width of the stele and the text. We use the measurements of line 13, we average the horizontal intervals of line 3, we assume that *Λύκο* is the correct patronymic in line 3; we then estimate that the length of line was 80 ± letters and the width of the stele 1.022 m. The patronymic *Λύκο*[*νος*], on the other hand, gives *ca* 90 letters to the line for the text proper and a width of 1.147 m. This implies, if our restoration of line 4 is correct, that the three names of the secretary, chairman, and orator demanded *ca* 33 letters, which, although possible, is not likely. We accordingly suppose that Meritt is right in reading *Λύκο* and estimating that each line contained about 80 letters.

Plate X. *I.G.*, I[2], 68/69, Athens and the Boiotians, reconstructed stele (fragments 2–5) (*Photograph courtesy of the National Epigraphic Museum*)

Plate XI. *I.G.*, I^2, 68/69, fragment 1, showing the molding (*Photograph courtesy of the National Epigraphic Museum*)

Plate XII. *I.G.*, I^2, 68/69, fragment 4 (*Photograph courtesy of the National Epigraphic Museum*)

Plate XIII. *I.G.*, I², 68/69, fragment 5 (*Photograph courtesy of the National Epigraphic Museum*)

[Θε]σ[πιôν]
[θ]ε[οί]
[Φιλέα]ς Λύκο [ἐγραμμάτευε]
[ἔδοχσεν τε̑ι βολε̑ι καὶ τȏι δ]έμοι, Αἰγεὶς ἐπρυτάνευε, [Νεοκλείδες ἐγραμμάτευε, . . . ±8 . . . ἐπεστάτε, . .]
[. . . . εἶπε· περὶ Θεσπιôν καὶ τ]ȏν ἄλλον Βοιοτôν ὅσοι βο[– –]
[. . . . . ca 25 . . . . ἑκάσ]τει τôν πόλεον ![– –]
[. . . . . 34-36 . . . .]ος Ἀθένεσι κα[– –]
[. . . ca 9 . . .]![. 3-4 .]![. . . . . ca 29 . . . .]αν[– –]
[.] ο[ἱ δὲ] Ἀθεναῖοι κ[– – – – – – – – – – – – – – – – 60-65 – – – – – – – – – – – – – – – – ὅπος δ']
[ἂ]ν ἐχ[σ]ε̑ι καὶ τὰ [ὀ]νό[μ]ατα ![– –]
[. 3-4 .]εόντον· ὅπος δ' ἂμ μὲ ἀ[δικε̑τ]αι μ[εδεὶς μέτε ὑπ' ἰδιότο μέτε ὑπ' ἄρχοντος Ἀθεναίον ἒ τôν χσυμμάχον]
[τ]ô[ν Ἀθε]ναίον ἐπιμελόσθον αὐτôν οἵτ[ινες Ἀθεναίον ἄρχοσιν ἐν τε̑ι ὑπερορίαι καὶ οἱ στρατεγοὶ οἳ ἂν]
[στρ]ατεγôσιν· καὶ ἐάν τι ἐσεγôντ[αι ἀγ]α[θὸν . 4-5 . .]ν αὐτο[– – – – – – – – – – – – – – – – – οἱ σ]
[τ]ρα[τεγ]οὶ ἐς τὲν βολὲν κα[ὶ] ἐς τ[ὸ]ν δ[ε̑μ]ο[ν καὶ κ]αταστεσά[ντον – – – – – – – – – – – – – – – – –]
ο ποόντ[ον τ]ά τ[ε] ἐπιτέδ[εια . . . . . 14-15 . . . . .]τα ἐν ὀφελίαι ![– –]
Θεσπιôν ὁς Ἀθενα[ιο . . . . . . ca 18 . . . . . . τὸν] δε̑μον ὁπότε[ρα –]
[. . .] οι[. . .]τον εἴτ[ε] ![. . .]τ[. . . . . 14-15 . . . . . ὁπότ]ερα δ' ἂν χειρο[τονε – – – – – – – – ὁ δε̑μος – – – – – – – – – – –]
[. . . 8-10 . . .]πα̅[. . . 8 . . . .]εντ[. . . . . 14-16 . . . . .]αι ὅπος ἂν κατ[– –]
[. . . . . ca 38 . . . .] οἱ δὲ στρατε[γοὶ –]
[. . . . . ca 37 . . . .]μ[. 4 . .]ονται [– –]
[. . . . . ca 44 . . . .]!υπ[– –]
[. . . . . ca 44 . . . .]ερ[– –]
[. . . . . ca 43 . . . .]α ἐὰν πο[– –]
[. . . . . ca 40 . . . .]\ο/[.]ΝΑ ἔθυσαν [– –]

[. . . . . ca 38 . . . .]ς δôν[α]ι̣ ἑκάστοι̣ [———————————————]
[ἔδοχσεν τε̂ι βολε̂ι καὶ τôι δέμοι . . 4–5 . . ὶς ἐπρυ]τάν̣[ε]υε Φιλ[έας] ἐγρ[αμμάτευε ———————————]
[. . . . . ca 35 . . . .]σοσ[———————————————————]
[. . . . . ca 33 . . . .]ο̣ν̣ μεδ[. . 4–5 . .]λ̣[———————————————]
[. . . . . ca 26 . . . . οἱ δὲ στρ]ατεγοὶ ἐχ[σ]ορκ[όντον ——————————————]
[ὅπος δ' ἂν ἅπαντες ὀμόσοσιν ἐπιμελόσθον] οἱ στρατεγοί· τὸ [δὲ φσέφισμα τόδε καὶ τὸ πρότερον ὃ . . ca 6 . .]
[εἶπε ἀναγραφσάτο ἐστέλεν λιθίνεν καὶ κα]τα[θ]έτο ἐμ πόλει ὁ [γραμματεὺς ὁ τε̂ς βολε̂ς ———————————]
[. . . . . ca 36 . . . .]ναι δὲ καὶ τοῖς ν[———————————————]
[. . . . . ca 39 . . . .]εσάντον δὲ [———————————————]
[. . . . . ca 37 . . . . φ]έ[ρο]σι καὶ ἄγοσ[ι ——————————————]
[. . . . . ca 41 . . . .]οροσιν ἐμμ̣[———————————————]
[. ca 43 . . . .] ε̣ρ̣αστε̣ [———————————————]

Line 1: The discovery of fragment 3 proves that this document concerns the Thespians and virtually confirms Meritt's acutely reasoned supplement [Θεσπιôν] in line 5, where other Boiotians are also under consideration. Since the Thespians are the principal subjects, we may expect to find their name inscribed as a heading on the analogy of, *e.g.*, *I.G.*, I², 57 (D3–6 in *A.T.L.*, II) and 86; Meritt, *Hesperia*, XIV (1945), pp. 109–10, had this in mind. The position of the surviving sigma in [Θε]σ[πιôν] agrees with the width of the stele as we have estimated it.

Line 3: For the secretary [Φιλέα]ς̣ see line 26. Again, the restored name precisely fits the reconstructed dimensions and the placement of the letters of line 3 spread across the width of the stele.

Lines 4–5: [Νεοκλείδες] West, *A.J.P.*, LVI (1935), p. 76, and Meritt, *op. cit.*, pp. 106–15. We accept Meritt's assignment of the document to 424/3, shortly after the battle of Delion, as the most plausible date, historically and epigraphically; in that year Neokleides was secretary of Aigeis (West, *op. cit.*, pp. 72–76). The second decree, passed when Phileas was secretary (lines 3 and 26), belongs to a later prytany. Since lines 14, 16, and 17 imply that decisions are to be made by the Boule and the *demos*, it is natural to expect no long interval between the two decrees; Phileas, perhaps, served in the next prytany. [περὶ μὲν Θεσπιôν καὶ τ]ô[ν ἄ]λλον Meritt. Attic decrees commonly begin without the particle; we therefore discard [μέν], thus allowing more space for the names of the *epistates* and the orator.

Lines 5–6: ὅσοι βο[εθέσαντες Ἀθεναίοις ἔφυγον τὲν σφετέραν αὐτôν | ἐ̑ναι γε̑ς ἔγκτεσιν καὶ οἰκίας (?) ἐν ἑκά]στει τôν πόλεον ἐς [---] Meritt. We believe that Meritt's restored relative clause (ὅσοι---αὐτôν) gives the desired sense. We also believe that Meritt is right in identifying the cities of line 6 as the cities of the empire, for we cannot conceive of the Athenians as having any formal relationship with the cities of Boiotia; the major concern is the Thespians, the "other Boiotians" are supplementary.

Perhaps Athens could grant the right of *enktesis* within the empire to her friends; but there is no specific evidence for this and we refrain from restoration. Pečírka, *The Formula for the Grant of Enktesis in Attic Inscriptions* (1966), pp. 4–8, rejects Meritt's text outright; he denies that "the Athenian assembly could have granted *enktesis* of anything else but *Athenian* land" (p. 8, n. 14). Pečírka, possibly, underestimates the will and power of the *demos*. We reject ἐς because there is no sigma on the stone; the preceding vertical could well be part of epsilon, or any other letter with a left-hand vertical.

Line 7: [ἄρχοντ]ος Ἀθένεσι Κα[λλιμάχο (?)] Hiller (*I.G.*, I^2). Kallimachos was archon in 446/5, which, we believe, is too early for the document; see above.

Lines 11–13: The restoration is essentially Meritt's.

Lines 13–14: ναυτο[δικ– – –] Meritt, who sees a reference to the *nautodikai*. The sense of this passage, we judge, is that under certain conditions (ἐάν) the generals are to introduce the Boiotian exiles into the Boule and the *demos*, *e.g.*, ἐάν τι ἐσεγôντ̣[αι ἀγ]α[θὸν ἒ δέο]ν αὐτο[ῖς ἒ Ἀθεναίοις πρόσοδον αὐτοῖς ποιεσάντον οἱ σ|τ]ρ̣α[τεγ]οί.

Lines 14–15: Perhaps [καθάπερ or ὅς προτ]|ô ποόντ̣[ον τ]ά̣ τ[ε ἐ]πιτέδ[εια Ἀθεναίοις καὶ ἄτ]τ̣α ἐν ὀφελίαι ἐ̣[στί].

Line 16: The surviving letters of line 17 imply that χειροτονêν or χειροτονêσαι should be restored before [τὸν] δêμον and that ὁπότε[ρα] is the following word. One would prefer the aorist infinitive in this context, in so far as we understand it; but the space is probably not available. The *demos* is to vote its preference concerning certain Thespians. The word ος̣ may represent ὡς or οὓς; the latter would demand a verb and again we should meet problems of space. What we therefore have in mind is something like this: [περὶ δὲ] | Θεσπιôν ὀς̣ Ἀθενα[ίοις φίλον χειροτονêν τὸν] δêμον ὁπότε[ρα– – –]

Line 17: [τôν] οἰ[κισ]τôν?

Line 24: The first alpha may be the relative ἅ. The first diagonal may be part of mu.

Line 26: The prytany is Oineis, Leontis, or Aiantis.

Line 28: [τε̂|ς Ἀθενᾶς τε̂ς Ἀθεν]ο̣̂ν̣ μεδ[εόσες] (or the dative)? Cf. the Decree of Themistokles, lines 4–5 (Jameson, *Hesperia*, XXXI [1962], pp. 310–15), and D15 in *A.T.L.*, II, pp. 68–69 = *I.G.*, I², 14–15, the Treaty with Kolophon, where in lines 13–14 the restoration should be [τε̂|ς Ἀθενᾶς τε̂ς] Ἀθενο̂ν μεδεόσ[ες] (Meritt).

Lines 29–31: We restore the first half of line 30 on the analogy of *I.G.*, I², 39 (D17, lines 16–20), the Treaty with Chalkis, and 19, lines 8–10, the Alliance with Egesta, in both of which the generals are given the responsibility of seeing that all swear. This leaves a gap of about thirty letters in line 29, part of which may be filled by μετὰ το̂ν *h*ορκοτο̂ν. The clause [κα]τα[θ]έτο ἐμ πόλει in line 31 implies a well-known formula; we take our restoration from the text prepared by Woodhead for *I.G.*, I³.

Line 36: [στατ]ε̂ρας τέ̣[τταρας] Hiller. Of the extant letters, sigma and tau are unmistakable, the two epsilons are quite certain (the horizontals and upper angles are identifiable), the triangular letter preceding sigma must be alpha; the second letter (the upper vertical and, probably, the beginning of the bow) is best interpreted as rho, although kappa is not impossible (in which case the supposed bow is not in fact a mason's cutting and the word is a form of ἕκαστος). We can find no justification for [στατ]ε̂ρας. Perhaps [ἑμ]έρας?

To judge from the width, this must have been a stele of considerable size. Comparatively, very little has survived, not sufficient, in fact, for us to derive a secure knowledge of the decrees. In the notes we have made a number of suggestions about individual passages, without insisting on their common coherence. Now, as we reflect on the text as a whole, we put forward one more proposal, as a question to readers rather than as an assertion.

In the note on line 17 we proffered [το̂ν] οἰ[κισ]το̂ν, which leads us to speculate that the Athenians, in their zeal to comfort the Thespians and the other pro-Athenian fugitives after the battle of Delion, might have planned to settle them as colonists somewhere in the empire, just as they were later to establish the Plataians in Skione. Compare Meritt's note (*op. cit.*, p. 113) on line 5: "... the assistance given the exiles included the privilege of settling down in any part of the Empire." We notice here the prominence of the generals (lines 13, 14, 19, 29, 30), who would naturally accept major responsibilities in the founding of colonies. Some of the provisions of the document (including, to be sure, our conjectures) recall those of the decree concerning a colony to Kolophon in 447/6 (D15):

	I.G., I^2, 68/69		D15
10.	*τὰ [ὀ]νọ́[μ]ατα*	31.	*[τὰ ὀ]νόματα*
17.	*[τôν] οἰ[κισ]τôν*	41.	*οἰκισταί* (cf. 19, 22)
24.	*ἃ* (?) *ἔθυσαν*	23.	*ἱερôν τôν παρ' α[ὐτοîς]*
25.	*δôν[α]ị ἑκάστọι* (money?)	24–25.	*ἕκαστος τêς ἑμ[έρας ἑκάστες ἐς ἐφόδια δραχμέν]*
28.	*[τêς Ἀθενâς τêς Ἀθεν]ộṇ μεδ[εόσες]*	13–14.	*[τêς Ἀθενâς τês] Ἀθενôν μεδεόσ[ες]*

CHAPTER V

Athens and Kolophon

(Plate XIV)

A re-examination of EM 2376, which contains parts of the opening lines of the decree concerning the Kolophonians, produced several new readings.[1] The stone is worn and battered, and thus very difficult to read. Many of the strokes appear only as orange patina on the yellowish stone and do not show up well on squeezes and photographs. The fragment must be examined in many different lights to distinguish all the traces remaining.

Our text is as follows:

447/6 B.C. *NON-ΣΤΟΙΧ.* 39–42

[*Ἔδοχσεν τε͂ι βολε͂ι καὶ το͂ι δέμοι, . . . ±9. . . . ἐπρυτά*]
[*νευε, . . . ±8. . .]ος̣ [ἐγραμμάτευε, . . ±7. . . ἐπεστάτε, ±2*]
[. .4. .] *ει̃π̣ε· Κ̣[ο]λ[ο]φ̣ο[ν*——————————————————]
[. . ±7. . .]*σ*[——————————————————————]
[. .4. .]*ες Ἀ̣θ̣ενα̣*[—————————————————————]
[. . .]*EONT*[. .] *αυτο*[———————————————————]
[.2-3.]*αι δὲ ταῦτα π* [—————————————————————]
[. .] *ἐ*[*χ*]*ς ἄλλες* [*π*]*όλ̣ε̣*[*ος* ——————————————————]
[. *Κ*]*ολο̣φο͂να ο*[*ἱ*] *π̣ο*[————————————————————]
[.2-3.] *κα̣τ*[—————————————————————————]

lacuna

[1] This fragment was added to *I.G.*, I², 14/15 (EM 6564 and 6564*a*), by Wade-Gery; *S.E.G.*, X, 17, lines 1–9, and *A.T.L.*, II, D15, with a photograph on Plate VIII. The latter text has slightly fuller readings than the former. See now Meiggs and Lewis, *G.H.I.* no. 47. We give a photograph on Plate XIV.

Plate XIV. EM 2376, now part of *I.G.*, I², 14/15 (D15), Athens and Kolophon (*Photograph by D. R. Laing*)

Line 1: The heading has heretofore been restored ἔδοξεν, since the use of xi could be expected in a text containing psi and no aspirates. But this now seems very unlikely, in view of line 8, where ἐ[χ]ς appears to be the only reasonable restoration. Meiggs and Lewis, *G.H.I.*, p. 122, argue for the use of xi because in line 53 "ἐχσόλες for ἐξόλες would give too long a line." It would, in fact, give a line of 41 letters, the same number as in lines 37, 38, and 54; and Meiggs and Lewis (p. 122) write "Non-stoichedon 39–42."

Line 2: [ἐγ]ρ̣α[μμάτευε] Wade-Gery. But the omicron seems certain and we see the lower stroke of sigma. The new readings demand a rearrangement of the spacing allowed for the names.

Line 3: [. . .]ς εἶπε· Κ̣[ο]λ̣[ο]φο̣[---] Wade-Gery. We cannot see the sigma but consider the lambda certain. The kappa is a left upright and of the phi only the top of the vertical stroke shows.

Line 6: The first epsilon is certain and there is a faint suggestion of a round letter after the first tau. A possible restoration is [πόλ]εον το̣͂[ν] αυτο͂[ν---]. We do not know whether the pronoun is reflexive or personal; the former is more likely.

Line 8: The first epsilon is sure and the reading almost certainly ἐ[χ]ς. πόλε̣[ος] Wade-Gery. We cannot see the pi; the upright of the lambda and the base of the epsilon survive in color.

Line 9: [. Κολο]φόνιο̣ι π̣ο[---] Wade-Gery (*S.E.G.*, X); [. Κ]ολ[ο]φόν̣ιοι πο[---] *A.T.L.*, II. In the ninth letter-space there is preserved, in color, most of an alpha. We can see no letter in the eleventh space, where the stone is badly broken. Only the upper right corner of the pi is visible, but the spacing suggests that there was an iota in the preceding *stoichos*.[2]

Line 10: We see the upper part of the vertical and the upper arm of kappa, the left side of alpha, all tau except the lower

[2] These readings for line 9, as well as those for line 10, have already been reported by McGregor, *Phoenix*, XXIV (1970), p. 181.

part of the vertical. These readings add a line and necessitate a renumbering of the lines that follow.

The new readings add little to our understanding of the opening lines of the decree, but the certain alpha in line 9 eliminates the basis of one of Mattingly's main arguments for associating this decree with the troubles at Kolophon from 430 to 427, namely, that Kolophon itself is not mentioned in the text.[3] Its appearance here shows that Athens controlled Kolophon itself at the time of this decree, as she did not in 427/6, and reinforces the commonly accepted date, *ca* 446, which is also indicated both by the letter-forms and by Kolophon's record of the payment of tribute.[4]

For the text of the other fragments as printed in *A.T.L.* we have no corrections except that in line 13 the reading should be [. . . . $\overset{9}{.}$ . . . . *Κο*]⟨*λ*⟩*οφονίον καὶ τõ*[*ν* ---]. The first preserved letter was inscribed as a delta, as noted by Hondius, *N.I.A.*, p. 15.

We feel, however, that the new edition of and commentary on this inscription by Meiggs and Lewis, *G.H.I.*, pp. 121–25, invite a reply. Their criticisms show that the exact wording and details of the oath, and of the lines introducing it, cannot be recovered; there are too many possibilities in these non-*stoichedon* lines. We believe, however, that the general sense of the restorations in *A.T.L.*, II, D15, is correct. Perhaps the allies were not mentioned in line 44, as Meiggs and Lewis maintain, but their argument that they cannot be included in the following negative clause will not stand. Line 46 could well

[3] *Historia*, X (1961), p. 175; XII (1963), pp. 266–67 (where lines 39–40 and 48 are restored with reference to Notion rather than Kolophon). In *A.S.&I.*, pp. 210–11, this argument is not invoked again, but rather one based upon a restoration that omits the allies from the oath (line 44), with a claim that this omission is evidence for a later date. Questions of restoration aside, the argument is worthless unless one believes Mattingly's wholly unacceptable date of 423 for the Chalkis decree of 446/5 (*I.G.*, I², 39), where too the allies are not in the oath. Meiggs and Lewis, *G.H.I.*, p. 125, while seriously questioning the restoration of the allies in the oath, still reject Mattingly's dating.

[4] See also Meiggs, *J.H.S.*, LXXXVI (1966), p. 96.

have read [λ]όγοι οὔτ' ἔργ[οι οὔτ' ἀπὸ τôν χσυμμάχον τôν Ἀθεναίον], the same wording as that in the Samian oath (*A.T.L.*, II, D18, lines 19–20). We should not, of course, insist upon this and agree with Meiggs and Lewis that this question has nothing to do with the dating and interpretation of the decree.[5] If mention of the allies is to be removed from lines 44–45, however, B. D. Meritt has suggested, *per litt.*, that [περὶ τὲν ἀποικί|α]ν[6] be substituted there for [περὶ τὸς ξυμμάχος αὐτ|ô]ν. This raises a far more important question of interpretation.

Meiggs and Lewis reject the view of the editors of the *A.T.L.* that the central portion of this decree deals with the establishment of a colony near Kolophon, although they misrepresent that view by describing it as "a colony of Athenians at or near Kolophon." "A colony of Athenians" is quite different from an Athenian colony. The editors say (*A.T.L.*, III, p. 282) of the composition of this colony: "Whether they colonized Kolophon with settlers from elsewhere in Asia Minor on whose loyalty they could depend, as Notion was later colonized with loyal Kolophonians, is not stated in the text of the inscription. But 'colonists' are named (line 22: [οἰκέτ]ορες), and it may well be that some of them were Athenian." We now suggest that the phrase ἐ[χ]ς ἄλλες [π]όλ̣ε̣[ος] in line 8 is a good indication that non-Athenians were included. Meiggs and Lewis argue against a colony: "Had an Athenian settlement been established at or near Kolophon as recently as 447 or 446 there should be some trace of it in Thucydides (iii. 34)." But Thucydides' account is summary and the argument has little weight if the colony contained a majority of non-Athenians. We have a good example of the attitudes in such a city in the case of Amphipolis, which showed little loyalty to Athens fifteen years after its founding.

More important, Meiggs and Lewis do not refute the main

[5] See above, note 3.

[6] This restoration produces only 37 letters in line 44, which would be unique. We propose [περὶ τὲν ἀποικίαν αὐτ|ô]ν.

argument for a colony, namely, the reduction in tribute for the Kolophonians and their neighbors, the Lebedioi and the Dioseritai. They cast doubt upon the parallel case of Erythrai, but present no explanation for the reductions in question nor for the fact that the Dioseritai certainly, and the Lebedioi most probably, are mentioned in our text along with the Kolophonians (lines 25–26). On their view, which seems to be that the text deals with a resettlement of Kolophonians at Kolophon, this reference to the neighbors owing money on the same basis as the Kolophonians is very strange. Until this reference and the reductions in the tribute can be explained, we believe that the case for a colony stands.

CHAPTER VI

The Proxeny-Decree *I.G.*, I², 149

(Plate XV)

A re-examination of *I.G.*, I², 149, revealed that frag. *a* (EM 6821) joined the top of frag. *b* (EM 6822). This diminishes the lacuna between the two to one line and makes obsolete previous restoration, which assumed a gap of three or five lines.[1] Our text is as follows:

430–415 B.C. *ΣΤΟΙΧ.* 25

["Εδοχσεν τε̂ι βολ]ε̂ι κ[αὶ τо̂ι δέμο]
[ι, . . . εὶς ἐπρυτ]άνευ[ε, . . ±6 . . ἐπ]
[εστάτε, . . ±6 . .]ς̣ ἐγρα̣[μμάτευε, .]
[– 6 or 8 – εἶπε, 3 or 1]υφεμ̣[2 or 4 καὶ 3 or 1]
[. . . . . . 13 . . . . .]αιον[. . καλέσα]
[ι τε ἐπὶ χσένια ἐ]ς τὸ πρ̣[υτανεῖο]
[ν καὶ ἐπαινέσαι h]ότι ν[ῦν ἄνδρε]
[ς ἀγαθοί ἐσιν περ]ὶ Ἀ̣θε[ναίος κα]
[ὶ ἐν τо̂ι πρόσθεν χρόνοι· . . 6 . . .]
[. . . . . 18 . . . .]τ̣[. .]σι[. .]
[. . . . . . . 16 . . . .]δε[. .]πρ̣[. . .]
[. . . . 10 . . . .]ο̣[. . · κα]ὶ̣ ὅς ἂ̣ν μὲ ἀ̣δ[ι]
[κε̂ται το]ῦ̣τ̣ον μ̣[ε]δἐ̣ς, hοι στρατε
[γοὶ hο]ὶ ἂν ὂσιν [ἑ]κ̣άστοτε καὶ hε
[βολὲ h]ε βολεύο[σ]α καὶ hοι πρυτά
[νες ἑκά]στοτε ἐ[πι]μελέσθον αὐτ̣

[1] Wilhelm, *Att. Urkund.*, IV, pp. 80–83 (*S.E.G.*, X, 105); Meritt, *Hesperia*, XXI (1952), pp. 344–46 (*S.E.G.*, XII, 29). See Plate XV.

Plate XV. *I.G.*, I^2, 149, showing the joins (*Photograph courtesy of the National Epigraphic Museum*)

[ὂν· τὸ δὲ φ]σ̣έφισ[μα] τόδε ἀνα[γραφ]
[σάτο ho γρ]αμμα[τε]ὺς ho τ̣[ε͂ς βολε͂]
[ς ἐν στέλει] λιθ[ίν]ει [καὶ καταθέ]
[το ἐμ πόλει]· ε͂να[ι δὲ καὶ εὐεργεσ]
[ίαν καὶ προ]χσε[νίαν αὐτοῖς καὶ]
[ἐκγόνοις------------]

A new study of this decree has been made by Michael B. Walbank in an unpublished dissertation entitled *Athenian Proxenies of the Fifth Century B.C.* (University of British Columbia, 1970), pp. 289–99; we have profited greatly from his discussion and wish to express to him our gratitude for making it available to us. We have in general followed his text for lines 1–9, except for slight changes in lines 4–5. We agree with him that the name in line 4 cannot be that of the archon Euphemos (417/6)[2] nor that of the orator of the decree.[3] If it were the latter, we should be left with 21 letter-spaces in lines 2 and 3 for the name of the secretary, which means that a demotic would have to be restored with the name there, something unexampled at this period.[4] In either case, there would not be enough room in the following sentence to include the reference to more than two honorands that seems to be required by the plural in line 13, as well as an ethnic, part of which may be preserved in -αιον (line 5).[5] Therefore this name must be that of one of the honorands, but even so there are difficulties caused by the lack of space. Walbank restores [. . .⁸. . . . εἶπε· Ε]ὔφεμ[ον καὶ . . . |

[2] So P. Haggard, *The Secretaries of the Athenian Boule in the Fifth Century B.C.* (New York, 1930), p. 20, n. 40; A. Raubitschek, *S.E.G.*, X, 105. The latter also states that this inscription was cut by the same hand as *I.G.*, I², 96, the Argive treaty of 417/6. The letter-forms on both are very similar, although of different sizes, but they also resemble closely those of *I.G.*, I², 944+, a casualty list usually dated to 431. We should reserve judgment whether they were by the same hand; even if they were, it would be no proof of date.

[3] So Kirchhoff, *I.G.*, I, *Suppl.*, p. 21, no. 76b; Wilhelm, *loc. cit.*; Meritt, *loc. cit.*

[4] See Meritt, *op. cit.*, p. 344, n. 8.

[5] Wilhelm, *loc. cit.*, restored two names, taking line 5 as [---κ]αὶ Ὂν[ασον], thus omitting the ethnic. Meritt, *loc. cit.*, objecting to this omission, restored only one name, ending in -αῖον, followed by an ethnic. He assumed that reference to the honorand's sons was included in the lacuna between the fragments, thus accounting for the plural. The new join eliminates this possibility.

. . . .⁹. . . . . τὸς Π]αίον[ας? καλέσα|ι], assuming only one more name; there is hardly room in twelve spaces for two more names and the necessary καί. We think it very unlikely, however, that two names would be followed by a plural rather than a dual; we can find no parallels at the time of this inscription.[6] We can see two other possibilities that will fit the space: either the -αιον of line 5 was part of a third name and there was no ethnic or the honorand had with him his sons, who were referred to but not named in the text. In the latter case the restoration could be [– –6 or 8– εἶπε· 3 or 1]υφεμ[όν τε καὶ τ|ὸς ὑες̂ αὐτο̂ τὸς Π]αίον[ας κτλ.] or, for the name itself, -υφεμ[ίδεν καὶ κτλ.]. A further complicating factor is the question of the name represented by what survives in line 4. All previous editors, even those who do not accept Euphemos as archon, have kept this name here. But, if this is not the archon, all certainty about the name disappears. It could as well have been Euphemides, Euthyphemos, Euryphemos, or Polyphemos (see Bechtel, *Personennamen*, p. 446).

From line 6 through most of line 9 the restoration is formulaic and seems mandatory. But the subject-matter from there on down to the middle of line 12 is not certain. Although the lacuna is technically of only one line (9), there are few sure letters in lines 10 and 11 and the first half of 12 because of the battered and weathered condition of fragments *b* and *c* in this area. In the nineteenth *stoichos* of line 10 earlier editors have reported tau, Walbank saw only an upper horizontal stroke, we could see nothing on the stone but thought we could make out a tau on the squeeze. In the twenty-second *stoichos* is the bottom stroke of a sigma; in the twenty-third the bottom of an upright, reported by all previous editors as central, but it is so close to the sigma (0.008 m.) that it must have been a left

[6] Cf. Meisterhans-Schwyzer³, pp. 199–200, where it is stated flatly that substitution of plural for dual is not found until after 409. For the dual in proxeny-decrees see *I.G.*, I², 154, lines 3, 6–8; II², 48, line 6; *S.E.G.*, X, 84, line 25 (the restoration of a plural in this decree in *I.G.*, I², 70, line 8, was shown to be an error by the discovery of a new fragment).

upright unless there was a stonecutter's error.[7] In line 11 the seventeenth and eighteenth letters are delta and epsilon, the twenty-first is pi, followed by a left upright. In the eleventh *stoichos* of line 12 previous editors have read an omicron, the outline of which we thought we could see in the eroded area; Walbank, however, reports the bottom of a central vertical in the ninth *stoichos*, an alpha in the tenth, and the bottoms of left and right verticals in the eleventh (ι̣αν̣). These few letters, most of them uncertain, are clearly not enough by themselves to give any clue to the subject-matter.

Wilhelm and Meritt, assuming a larger lacuna, restored here a guarantee of access to the Boule and *demos*. This might logically be expected, even though the provisions of this decree were drawn up in an unusual order.[8] Walbank retains this subject-matter by restoring in lines 9–13: [πρόσοδ|ον δὲ καὶ ἐ͂ναι αὐτοῖσι] π̣[ρὸ]ς τ̣[ὲμ | βολέν· προσαγόντον] δὲ [οἱ] πρ̣[υτά|νες οἳ αἰε]ὶ̣ ἂν̣ [ὄσι]ν̣· *hos* ἂν μὲ ἀδ[ι|κε͂ται]. For the first sentence he offers as an alternative an abbreviation of Wilhelm's and Meritt's text, [πρόσοδ|ον δὲ ἐ͂ναι αὐτοῖσι πρό]τ̣[οι]σι̣ [με|θ' ἱερά], but points out that there is no parallel for the omission of a reference to the Boule or *demos*. We believe that both versions of the first sentence are unacceptable because of the position of the upright after the sigma in line 10. We have grave doubts about the second sentence because of the position of ἄν in its clause and the lack of a connective (καί) before the following sentence. The only supplement we can find to retain here a reference to access to the Boule, which at the same time fits the traces we see in line 10, is: [αἰεὶ δὲ πρὸς τὲμ βολὲν ἐ͂ναι αὐ]τ̣[οῖ]ς π̣[ρό|σοδον· προσαγόντον] δὲ [οἱ] πρ̣[υτά|νες οἳ ἄν λάχ]ο̣[σι· κα]ὶ̣ ὅς ἂν μὲ ἀδ[ι|κε͂ται].[9] We realize that the contorted order of the first sentence

[7] In the tenth and eleventh spaces of line 14 the lower tip of the sigma is 0.013 m. from the iota; in the sixteenth and seventeenth spaces of the same line the sigma is 0.015 m. from the base of the tau.

[8] The invitation, usually late, occurs first (lines 5–6); the grant of *proxenia* comes unexpectedly late (lines 20–22).

[9] In line 12, Wilhelm's [νες οἳ ἂν ἀεὶ] ὅ[σι· κα]ί is also possible, but we doubt the shortened spelling of ἀεί; cf. Wade-Gery, *J.H.S.*, LI (1931), p. 83.

makes it suspect and that we have ignored Walbank's new readings in line 12. Taken together, these two factors support the conjecture that the subject-matter here is something quite different, perhaps a designation of some of the honorands' good deeds, and that therefore restoration is impossible until we reach the formulae beginning in line 12.

CHAPTER VII

Adnotationes Epigraphicae

(Plates XVI–XXIV)

In the course of several months of continuous study in the Epigraphical Museum we examined hundreds of fragments, whenever feasible collating the readings with the published text. For about a decade after 1939 Athens was inaccessible to epigraphists. During that period much significant work was carried out and published, especially by B. D. Meritt, as the pages of *Hesperia* testify. This was done on the basis of squeezes and photographs, with the realization that readings and joins were subject to confirmation when the stones once more became susceptible to autopsy. Much of this testing has of course been accomplished; there remain, however, a few texts in which improvements or corrections should be noted.

We have included in this chapter only those observations that seem to us to possess some special importance or interest. Others, of a more trifling nature, will eventually be incorporated in the projected third edition of *Inscriptiones Graecae*, I.

Where no other edition is specified, we collate by *Inscriptiones Graecae*, I^2.

I.G., I^2, 12/13*a*: EM 6562

We collate by D10 in *A.T.L.*, II, p. 56, with a photograph on Plate III. The left edge is not preserved (*pace* Hiller). In line 73 we read the first letter as omicron; we see the right side. The

Plate XVI. *I.G.*, I^2, 29 (*Photograph courtesy of the National Epigraphic Museum*)

Plate XVII. *I.G.*, I[2], 34 fragments *a* and *b* (*Photograph courtesy of the National Epigraphic Museum*)

Plate XVIII. *I.G.*, I², 35, lines 12–23 (reverse surface of *I.G.*, I², 34) (*Photograph courtesy of the National Epigraphic Museum*)

Plate XIX. *I.G.*, I², 35, lines 1–11 (= fragment *c*) (*Photograph courtesy of the National Epigraphic Museum*)

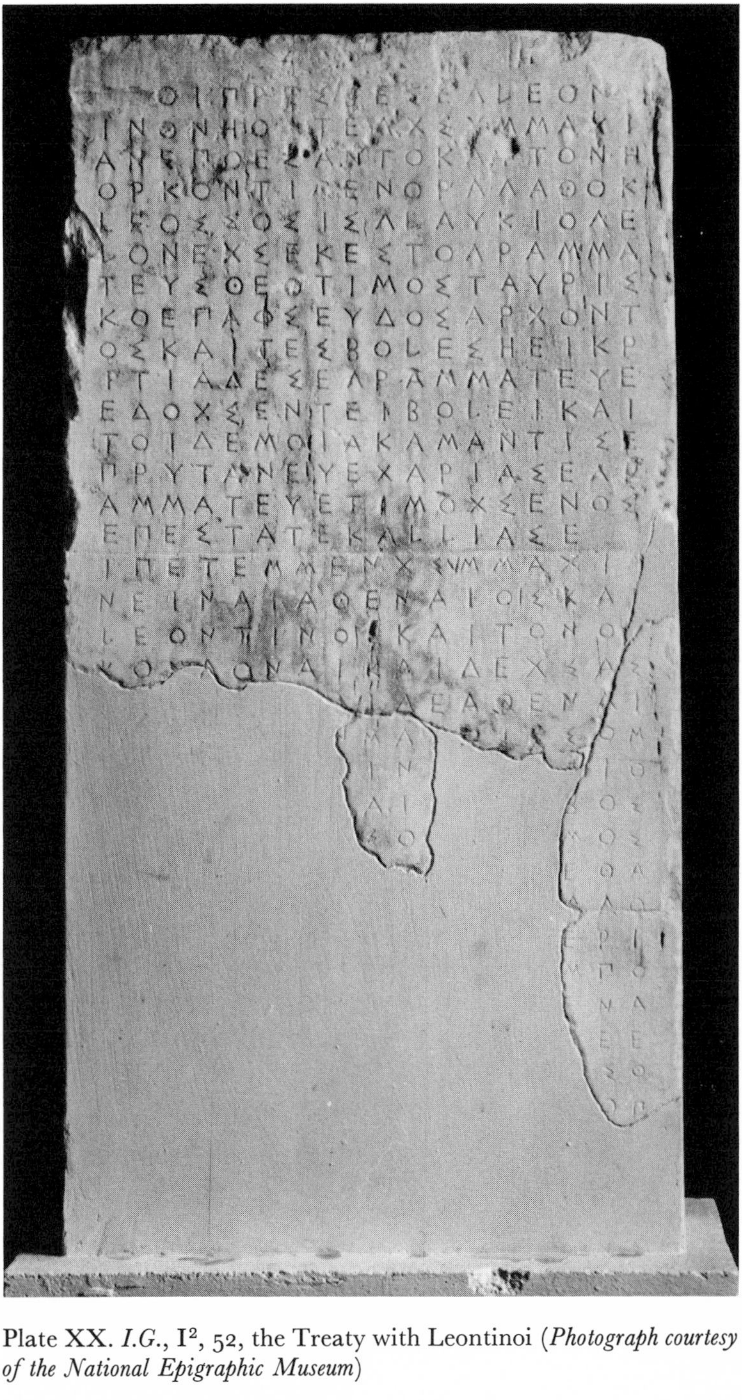

Plate XX. *I.G.*, I², 52, the Treaty with Leontinoi (*Photograph courtesy of the National Epigraphic Museum*)

Plate XXI. *I.G.*, I^2, 60, fragment *f*, now in the Musée du Louvre
(*Photograph courtesy of the Musée du Louvre*)

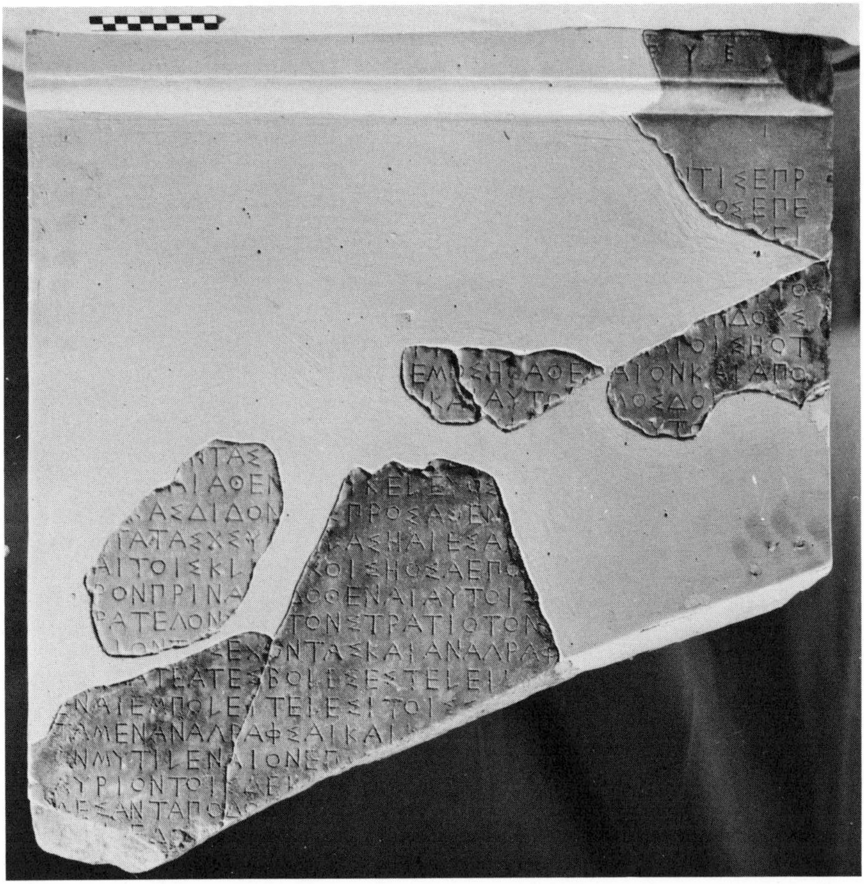

Plate XXII. *I.G.*, I^2, 60, the Treaty with Mytilene, as reconstructed
(*Photograph courtesy of the National Epigraphic Museum*)

Plate XXIII. *I.G.*, I², 87, the Treaty with Halieis (without the fragment now in Cambridge) (*Photograph courtesy of the National Epigraphic Museum*)

Plate XXIV. *I.G.*, I², 101

disposition of the text as previously given is inaccurate. The restoration is sound but we cannot determine where each line begins and ends. At least one letter must be shifted from the ends to the beginnings of the lines. In the present state of our knowledge lines 72–73, for example, are best printed as follows:

[ο]ν τôν Ἀθεν[αίο]ν́ οὔτ' αὐ[τὸς ἐγὸ οὔτ' ἄλλοι πείσομαι, τε̂ι δὲ γν]
ό[μ]ει τε̂[ι] Ἀθ[ε]ναίον πείσ[ομαι· ἀναγράφσαι δὲ ταῦτα καὶ τὸν h].

I.G., I², 16: EM 6918

We collate by Meiggs and Lewis, *G.H.I.*, no. 31, and report the following readings.

Line 2: *Ἀκαμαντί[ς].*

Lines 3–4: *[. . .]σιππος ἐγ[ραμ]μάτευεν, 'Ε*
[πιμ]ή̣δης.

Line 6: *μέν̣.*

Line 14: *τ[ά]ς; ε̂ναι.*

Line 19: *ἄκ[υ]ρ̣ος.*

Line 20: *[παραβ]α[ίν]ηι.*

Line 21: *[ὀφε]λέ̣[τ]ω.*

Line 23: *τό[δ]ε.*

I.G., I², 26: EM 6807

We collate by *S.E.G.*, XIII, 3 (Meritt, *A.J.P.*, LXXV [1954], pp. 369–73).

Line 2: The final letter, now read as iota, may have the trace of a horizontal at the top right; it is to the left of the *stoichos*. It could be a pi; whatever is printed should be dotted.

Line 4: The first visible letter is a vertical stroke, firmly cut on good surface. It has caused trouble because it produces a name, [. .⁵. .]*ίες*, that no one has been able to restore satisfactorily. Hiller read [. .⁵. .]*ν̣ες*, but the nus in this inscription slant. The stroke is cut at the extreme left of the *stoichos*, unlike the other iotas. Thus it is not unlikely that the letter is unfinished, *i.e.*, it was intended as, *e.g.*, lambda, rho, or kappa. The apparatus in *S.E.G.*, XIII, 3, suggests *[Περικ]⟨λ⟩ε̂ς* (Meritt), which is reasonable epigraphically.

Line 6: ἀπ[αγγ]. The second alpha is not visible.

I.G., I², 27 (*S.E.G.*, X, 19; XII, 9; XXI, 15)

We are not convinced that frag. *b* (EM 56) goes with frag. *a* (EM 6569). The chequer of *a* measures 0.0275 m. horizontally, that of *b* 0.030 m. There are so few letters extant in the latter that certainty is impossible.

Line 9: The lambda of πόλε[ι] was corrected from epsilon.

We read frag. *b* as follows:

.O
TO
IΔ/
X𐅃
vacat

I.G., I², 28*a*: EM 7013

We collate by *S.E.G.*, X, 23 (Wilhelm).

Line 2: [ε]ὐεργέτ̣ε̣[ν] BM. We prefer Meritt's τινον to Wilhelm's τινος (see the plural in line 4).

Lines 6–7: δραχμ[ôν] Meritt and McGregor. In our commentary on the Regulations for Miletos (p. 43, n. 21, above) we have shown why [μεδὲ τἀπιδέκατα] is impossible. We propose [τὸν γραφσάμενον] (the plaintiff, not necessarily Acheloion).

Lines 8–9: For Wilhelm's τιν[ὰ ἐν τôν πόλεόν πο | ὁπό]σον Ἀθεναῖο[ι κρατôσιν] we prefer τιν[ὰ ἔν τινι τôν πόλε|ον ὅ]σον Ἀθεναῖο[ι κρατôσιν].

Lines 11–13: Walbank has convinced us that the relationship between the lines is wrongly presented. So the restoration is nullified. In fact, the nus of lines 10, 11, and 12 all fall in the same vertical *stoichos*, as does the theta of line 13. We suggest:

[γραφὲν δὲ Ἀθέν]
[εσι ἐ̃]ναι κατὰ τ[ὸ αὐτὸ ὅσπερ Ἀθεναί]
[ο ἀπο]θανόν̣[τος ——————————]

We might perhaps read κατὰ τ[ούτο hόσπερ], except that the

daseia appears not to have been employed in this document; see lines 2 ([ὑπό]), 9 ([ὅ]σον), and 10 ([ὅς]).

I.G., I^2, 29: EM 6565
(Plate XVI)

We collate by *I.G.*, I^2, 29. For the two pieces found in the Agora see Meritt, *Hesperia*, XIV (1945), pp. 83–85.

In line 7 we read *μεδένα̣ [κ]α̣θιστα*. Of the first alpha the very tip of the apex is detectable and of the second the right side and the apex.

I.G., I^2, 34/35: EM 6571, 6613
(Plates XVII–XIX)

I.G., I^2, 34 (EM 6571), consists of two joining fragments, broken on all sides, denoted as *a* and *b* by Hiller; see Plate XVII. The reverse of these opisthographic pieces bears lines 12–23 of *I.G.*, I^2, 35; see Plate XVIII. EM 6613 (= *I.G.*, I^2, 35, lines 1–11, identified as *c* by Hiller) belongs but does not join; the right side is preserved, as Plate XIX demonstrates.

The two fragments of EM 6571 are faultily joined in the Epigraphic Museum, as a glance at Plates XVII and XVIII, especially the latter, will confirm.

The size of type employed in *I.G.*, I^2, is meant to indicate that the letters of lines 1–3 of no. 35 are taller and more widely spaced than the letters of lines 4–23. This is an optical illusion. In fact, the letters of line 1 are, comparatively, tall (height 0.014 m., lateral chequer 0.0185 m.) and widely spaced whereas those of lines 2–3 form a *stoichedon* pattern with lines 4–22 (height 0.0105 m., lateral chequer 0.011 m.). Below line 22 the mason left an uninscribed space 0.015 m. in depth and the letters of line 23 (see the note *ad loc.*) are of the same height, approximately, as those of line 1 and widely spaced. The two surfaces were not inscribed by the same mason; the sigma of no. 34 is distinctive and three-barred, that of no. 35 four-barred.

We add a few adjustments in the readings, taking *I.G.*, I^2, 34 first.

Line 6: [. .⁴. .] ἐάν; part of the top horizontal of epsilon remains. Rho, having been omitted originally, was inserted between omicron and kappa.

Line 9: [. . .⁷ . . .ο]ντος; while it is true that the fracture is circular, we can find no chiselled trace of omicron.

Line 10: [. . .⁶ . . Δε]μοχάρ̣ος; a mere trace of the vertical of rho may be identified on the upper fragment.

Lines 14–15: We cannot see the final letters (omicron and lambda) read in *I.G.*, I², but a chip of stone may have broken away recently.

Line 3: The last three letters, ATE, occupy two crowded *stoichoi*.

Line 16: HOι; the vertical is centered.

Line 21: [. . .⁷ . . .] ἀ̣ργύ̣ριον κ[---]. On the lower fragment one can see the lower right-hand tip of alpha, all the rho, all the gamma, and the top of the vertical of upsilon. Here too the flaw in the join may best be observed; see Plate XVIII.

Line 23: [. . . . . .]ΟΙ̣Σ.ΣΥΜ[---].

I.G., I², 46: EM 6810

The stele is opisthographic and was inscribed by two masons, one for each surface. We revise the readings of *I.G.*, I².

Line 17: Omicron is followed by a left-hand sloping lower tip, probably of nu.

Line 18: We see no tau.

Line 19: Read ἐπειδάν.

Line 20: The vertical of phi and the cutting of the circle at top and bottom survive. Sigma needs no dot.

Line 22: The last two letters are AP.

Line 23: Read ἐ̣π̣ειδάν; the vertical of epsilon and the horizontal of pi are on the stone.

Line 25: The final alpha is not present.

Line 26: We see no initial tau; the apparent cutting is a mirage, too far to the right.

Line 29: Read [π]ρέσβες.
Line 30: Read [γ]ράφσονται.

I.G., I², 50 (*A.T.L.*, II, D18): EM 6623, 6623β,5408, 6623α

We collate by Meiggs and Lewis, *G.H.I.*, no. 56.

Line 2: The vertical of the last extant letter is to the left of the *stoichos* and may not be iota.

Line 3: The letter after IKE may be epsilon; the beginnings of a bottom horizontal are visible.

Line 6: οι καταṣ[.

Line 13: ἀποδọ[.

Line 17: ἀγαθόν.

Lines 21–22: We note the restoration [δρ]άσο καὶ ἐρô καὶ | [βολεύσο καλὸν τôι δέμοι τôι] Σαμίον. Bradeen, *Historia*, IX (1960), pp. 265–66 with note 48, observed that Thucydides' account of the settlement of the Samian revolt (I, 117, 3: the Samians προσεχώρησαν ὁμολογίạ), "taken naturally, would imply no change in the surrendering government, which was an oligarchy." In 412 B.C. the incumbent government of Samos was oligarchic (Thucydides, VIII, 21) and it has been assumed that at some time between 439 and 412 there had been an oligarchic revolution, countenanced by the Athenians; *A.T.L.*, III, p. 151. The evidence for the establishment of democracy in 439 seems to lie in these lines and in Diodoros, XII, 28, 4. J. P. Barron, *The Silver Coins of Samos*, pp. 80–93, in an attempt to establish a chronological framework for the Samian coinage, posits an oligarchy from 454/3 to 439, democracy until 413/2, and a short-lived oligarchy in that year. But his reconstruction and chronology bristle with difficulties and we believe that he has been decisively refuted by E. Will, *Rev. ét. anc.*, LXXI (1969), pp. 305–19. The latter maintains that Samos was ruled by an oligarchy from the time of the Persian Wars until 412, except for the brief interlude in 441/0. We therefore propose that the text should read [τêι πόλει τêι] Σαμίον, on the understanding that Athens came to terms with the oligarchs and allowed oligarchic government to continue.

Line 31: [ν]ε̣ίδος Χ̣σ̣ε̣[νοφôν Κεκροπίδο]ς.

Lines 32–33: For Ἀ̣θ[εν|αίοις hε̂ι] see *A.T.L.*, IV, p. x.

I.G., I², 52: EM 6855, 6855α (Plate XX)

The treaties with Rhegion (*I.G.*, I², 51) and Leontinoi (*I.G.*, I², 52) were restudied by Meritt, *Class. Quart.*, XL (1946), pp. 85–91, and are published as nos. 63 (Rhegion) and 64 (Leontinoi) by Meiggs and Lewis, *G.H.I.*

Four fragments (EM 6855) are built into a stele in the Epigraphic Museum; the fifth (EM 6855α) is reported by Meritt but not by Meiggs and Lewis (it preserves seven letters in three lines and makes no join with other fragments).

In lines 16, 17 and 18 letters were added between *stoichoi* and Meritt reasonably posits similar corrections in lines 21 and 22; these irregularities do not appear in Meiggs and Lewis, *G.H.I.*

Line 1: [Θ]εοί Hiller, Meiggs and Lewis; Θεοί Meritt. The stone-cutter originally inscribed ΘΕΟΙ:ΓΡΕΣΒΕΣ. He then erased ΘΕ and the punctuation; we were meant to read ΟΙΓΡΕΣΒΕΣ; see McGregor, *Phoenix*, XXIV (1970), p. 181. His erasure was not executed neatly and the tops of theta and epsilon as well as the punctuation remain visible.

Line 32: The final letter is demonstrably pi (Meritt), not tau (Hiller, Meiggs and Lewis).

I.G., I², 60 (*A.T.L.*, II, D22): EM 6823, 6823α, 6823β, 6631 (Plates XXI and XXII)

Fragment *f* of *I.G.*, I², 60, now in the Louvre and illustrated in *A.T.L.*, II, Plate XV, does not belong with the other seven fragments; see Plates XXI (fragment *f*) and XXII (the seven fragments joined in plaster). Fragment *f*, of Pentelic marble, with a sculpted Athena above, has Ionic lambda and eta

(ΜΥΤΙΛΗ[---]); the other fragments are of darkish marble and the orthography is uniformly Attic. Fragment *c* lacks any trace of mortise and anathyroses for the tenon of fragment *f*.

We found in the Epigraphic Museum at Athens that fragment *e* (EM 6823α) consisted of two joined pieces (see the lower illustration in *A.T.L.*, II, Plate XV); that fragment *a* (EM 6631) had been joined to and bore the same inventory number as the two fragments published as *d* (see the lowest illustration in *A.T.L.*, II, Plate XVI); that fragments *c* (EM 6823) and *b* (EM 6823β) rested independently on the shelves. A series of joins links the fragments securely together. Before describing these, we set out the new numbers that will be used in *I.G.*, I³, to designate these fragments. We move from the top and from left to right.

c = 1
e = 2, 3
b = 4
a = 5
d = 6, 7

Fragments 1 and 4 have preserved right sides and in fact join at the extreme edges; fragment 4, at its left tip, also joins fragment 3. The latter sits snugly against its left-hand neighbor, fragment 2. Fragment 2 in its turn joins the top of fragment 7. On its upper left fragment 7 joins fragment 5 (behind the surface and so not visibly in the photograph) while on its lower left it fits perfectly alongside fragment 6. Fragment 6 at the top is securely attached to fragment 5.

The text of *A.T.L.*, II, D22 shows the correct relationships. We had all the fragments set in plaster and we publish a photograph in Plate XXII.

Lines 12–13: δοκ[εῖ] ἐ̂ν|[αι]. The top and bottom horizontals and the vertical of epsilon are in part detectable.

I.G., I², 70: EM 5186, 8184, 254

Collating by *S.E.G.*, X, 84, we revise the readings as follows:

Line 6: [πρυτάν]ες π̣ρός.

Line 9: Ẹ O . I.

Line 12: There is no trace after ATELE.

Line 21: εὑρέσθ̣α̣[ι]. There is nothing inside the circular letter. Alpha is represented by the lower left-hand tip.

Line 29: hοι κολα.

Line 30: το δ̣[έ].

Line 32: δε̂μ̣ον. The right-hand stroke with the top angle of mu is visible.

Line 35 (init.): ον.

Line 36: αὐτôν [ἀ]π̣. The left-hand vertical of pi is present.

Line 38: [κπ]ράττοντε[ς].

Line 40: αὐτοκ̣[ράτορ]. We see the vertical of kappa.

Line 44: hαύριον̣. The lower tip of the left hasta of nu is detectable.

Line 48: POHOT^.

I.G., I², 87: EM 6799, 6819, 2727, Fitzwilliam Museum Gr 36–1865 (Plate XXIII)

The treaty with Halieis was revised by Meritt, *Hesperia*, XIV (1945), pp. 97–105 (*S.E.G.*, X, 80), who noted that in line 34 (his 33, but his text does not include line 1: [Θεο]ί) the "letters NEON are out of their *stoichoi* and no letter can be restored immediately either before or after them" (p. 99); he reads ^{v} *Νέον* ^{v} Ἀ[. .]. In fact, the alpha is also well to the left of its *stoichos* and its placement was probably influenced by the irregularity discussed by Meritt. The latter observes that in line 5 the letters ΓΕΧΣΥ occupy four *stoichoi* and we draw attention to a similar crowding in line 26, where the letters NEI are forced into two *stoichoi*. Meritt assumes that in line 32 the final iota and initial epsilon of [θε̂ναι ἐμ] were cut in a single *stoichos*. The document is thus *stoichedon* 42.

Line 8: [α]ὐτό̣ς̣

Line 28: αὐτοῖς Ἀ[θεναίον].

I.G., I², 97: EM 6590, 6634

We collate by Meritt, in *Studies Presented to David Moore Robinson*, II (St. Louis, 1953), pp. 298–303.

Lines 2–5: Our readings of the stone lead to the following proposed restoration:

> [. . .⁷. . . τὲν δὲ βολὲν ἐχσενεγκ]ệν ἐπάναγκε[ς ἐς τὸν δε̂μο]
> [ν αὐτίκα μάλα περὶ τô φόρο καὶ τ]ôν ἐπιφορôν [hίνα hοι χσύ]
> [μμαχοι τελôσιν τὰ ὀφελόμενα ἐ]ντελε̂ καὶ τὸμ π[όλεμον χσ]
> [υνδιαπολεμôσιν πρὸς Πελοπονν]εσίος καθότι χρ[εστὰ . .]

Line 6: [. . . . . .²³. . . . .]εον.

Line 18: [χσυ]μμ⟨ά⟩χον. The horizontal of alpha was not cut.

Line 33: [. . .⁷. . .]τον BM; [. . .⁷. . .]ρον Meritt, whose photograph (Plate 69) is misleading. The vertical and much of the horizontal of tau, including all the right side, are clear on the stone.

I.G., I², 101: EM 6592, 6592α (Plate XXIV)

David M. Lewis, *B.S.A.*, XLIX (1954), p. 29: "It even seems reasonably certain that the two fragments join. Although they do not make a perfect fit, the surfaces are so consistent over so large an area that I am confident they must join. . . ." We confirm Lewis's words and have had the two fragments set in plaster. There is no doubt whatever about the join, as was apparent when they were placed on their sides against one another; the join is at the back and does not show on the photograph.

I.G., I², 105: EM 6644

We collate by Meritt's text, in *Classical Studies Presented to Edward Capps* (Princeton, 1936), pp. 246–52 (*S.E.G.*, X, 138; Meiggs and Lewis, *G.H.I.*, 91).

Line 6: {τ̣[ȏ]ν} BM; ν[ȗ]ν Meiggs and Lewis; ν̣[ȗ]ν *priores*. What we see of the first letter is most of a vertical stroke, centered beneath tau in the line above; it does not suit nu. The squeeze suggests a horizontal and the break in the next *stoichos* is circular. We therefore believe that the mason committed a simple dittography.

Line 14: [δ]έ. Parts of all horizontals are detectable.

Lines 15–16: ἐγ. Again, the horizontals are visible in part. στ̣|[έλλοσι]. The left side of the horizontal remains.

Line 16: [ἐπι]μελεθε̂ναι.

Line 23: [κ]αθάπ[ερ].

Line 25: [χρ]ό̣ν̣οι.

Line 34: [εὐεργέτεκ]εν.

Line 37: [ἐστέλεν λιθίνε]ν BM; [ἐστέλεν λιθίνεν] Meritt; [ἐστέλει λιθίνει] *S.E.G.*, X, Meiggs and Lewis. The two tips of the uprights of nu are visible and allow us to confirm Meritt's restoration.

I.G., I², 106: EM 6624, 6624α, 6604 (four pieces)

Line 11: The lambda is Attic (*pace* Hiller); there are some Ionicisms in the document, *e.g.*, ξυνβουλεύσοντ[ας] (19).

Line 12: [στρ]ατεγός.

Line 17: Πειραιᾶ.

I.G., I², 107: EM 6824

The spacing of line 7, inaccurately printed in *I.G.*, I², is: I. . .P.ΣΟΠOLE.

Line 9: ΡΟΘΥΜ̣ΟΤΑ̣. Mu is indicated by a right-hand diagonal and alpha by the angle at the apex.

Line 13: Ο.ΣΤΑΤΕΜΕ. The mu occupies two *stoichoi*. Sigma falls below the rho of line 7.

Line 15: We see only ΤΑΤΕ immediately below the same letters in line 13.

Line 16: We see no traces.

I.G., I², 108: EM 6598, 6589

The decrees of the Athenians honoring the Thracian Neopolitai were revised by Meritt and Andrewes, *B.S.A.*, XLVI (1951), pp. 200–209 (*S.E.G.*, XII, 37; Meiggs and Lewis, *G.H.I.*, no. 89). We offer a number of minor corrections in the text. There are nine fragments all told, eight (EM 6598) built into a stele (see the photograph in Meritt and Andrewes, Plate 23) and a small one (EM 6589) that makes no join (Meritt and Andrewes, photograph on p. 200).

Line 5: Σιβυρτιάδη[ς].

Line 21: [Ἀθ]ηνα[ιο---]. We see no sign of theta.

Line 32: βου̣λόμενοι. The upright of upsilon is visible.

Line 47: Δεκελεεῖ στρατεγôι. Three letters are crowded *in rasura* (the lettering is non-*stoichedon*).

Line 59: [ά]φ̣σαι, ἀποικία̣[ς]. We see the top of the vertical of phi, the apex of alpha.

Lines 59–60: [πρέ|σβεσι δὲ . .]αι Meritt and Andrewes (see also Hiller); [. . . | . . .^{11}. . .]σ̣αι BM. The upper stroke of sigma is clear and the restoration is unsupportable. Perhaps]σ̣αι is preceded by a name.

I.G., I^2, 124: EM 6928

In line 1 the left tip of Ionic lambda is quite clear. There is scarcely room for three letters after lambda and we rearrange the division of letters in the first two lines. This means that [Σ]ωτίων will not do for the name. We prefer:

> [Ἐρ]ωτίων ἐγραμμάτευεν Ἐλ[ευ]
> [σί]νιος.

I.G., I^2, 125: EM 2792, 255, 3169

Line 2: [Π]όλυπος. The fifth letter is not beta; the horizontal and a tip of the small vertical make pi a certain reading.

Line 3: [πρ]όξενος.

Line 7: [πρόξ]ενος.

Line 8: There is no omicron in the second letter-space.

I.G., I^2, 305: EM 6705, 6705α, 6781

Fragment *c* joins *b*; *a* all but joins *b*. The disposition of the fragments in *I.G.* is correct (non-*stoichedon*). The lacuna in lines 1 and 2 is of about 27 letters, in line 3 of about 24, in line 4 of about 23. We adjust the text as follows:

Line 5: [. . .ca 6. . .]α[. . .ca 6. . . καὶ συνάρχ]οσιν.

Line 6: γ[υ]ρα[σ]ίωι [. . . . . .ca 11. . . . . ὀ̣]γδόει φθί[νοντος].

Line 7: η̣ι φθίνον[τ]ος.

Line 8: ἀθλοθ[έταις].

Line 9: Προκ[λ]έει.

Line 10: Πατρο[κ]λ̣[εῖ], τρίτ[ηι].

Lines 11–12: [Ἀθηναίαι] | Ν̣[ί]κει Meritt, McGregor. κεφά[λ]-αιον.

Line 13: π̣[α]ρέδομε[ν].

Lines 13–14: [τε|τά]ρτει [φ]θίνο̣ν̣[τ]ος Μουνιχ̣[ιῶνος].

Line 15: [. . . Κ]υ̣ζι̣[κηνοὶ σ]τατῆρες^{v} $\overset{\Delta}{\Sigma}$.

Line 16: [. . . ἀ]ργύ̣[ρι]ον.

Line 17: ΗΔΔΔIIII.

Line 19: Ἀθε[ναίας] preceded by a *vacat*. The first numeral ($\overset{\Delta}{\Sigma}$) was seen by Köhler but has perished.

I.G., I^2, 311 (at Eleusis)

We report a few improvements in the text.

Line 6: χσυναρχόντο[ν].

Line 8: προ̑[τος].

Lines 10–11: Φι[λ]όστρατο[ς] Κ[υδαθεναι|εὺς] ἐγραμ̣μάτευε.

Line 13: [κα]ί; [ἀργ]ύ[ρι]ον (the left diagonal of upsilon).

Line 14: θ[εο]ῖν.

Line 15: Χαρῖνος; the lowest stroke of sigma survives.

Line 21: [ἀ]παρχε̑ς.

Line 22: [προ̑τ]ος ἐγραμμάτευε.

A.T.L., I and II, List 1

In V, 13 the mason cut ϟΙΝΔΙΟΙ and we should print Σίν⟨γ⟩ιοι.

A.T.L., I and II, List 25

There are two flaws in the prescript as restored in *A.T.L.* The line is too long and the relationship between lines 3 and 4 is falsely represented. We compute the width of the stele as 0.905 m. and the lateral measurement of the chequer as 0.013 m. These dimensions suit a line of 65 letters (= 0.845 m.) and an allowance of 0.060 for margins. In relationship to line 3, line 4 must be shifted one *stoichos* to the left. The prescript now reads as follows:

ΣΤΟΙΧ. 65

[ἐπὶ τε̂ς πέμπτες καὶ εἰκοστε̂ς ἀρχε̂ς hε̂ι ....22..........
ἐγραμματευε]

[hελλενοταμίαι ἐ̂σαν ....48............
..........]

[...............34................Δι]ο[νύ]σιο[ς Ἀχαρ]νεύς,
[......14......]

[....10.... Ἀχερδό]σιος, Αἴσχρον Μαραθόνιος, Φιλοτάδες
Παλλε[νεύς. *vacat*]

We revise the readings in the Hellespontine group of III, 36–39:

[Νεάπολι]ς
[Νε]αν̣δ[ρειε̂]ς
Ἀρισβαι̂οι
Πρίαπος

The lowest hasta and part of the lower angle of sigma in [Νε]αν̣δ[ρειε̂]ς can in fact be seen in the photograph in *A.T.L.*, I, fig. 125 (p. 93). This spelling of the name, rather than Νεάνδρεα or Νεάνδρεια, occurs in Lists [22] and 23 and A9 and [A13]; it is thus more likely in List 25.

A.T.L., II, D23: EM 2634, 2635, 6854β, 6854γ, 6829, 6626, Ag. Inv. No. I 2806

Photographs of this decree (Agora Inv. No. I 2806 plus *I.G.*, I², 144 *d, a, b* and *I.G.*, I², 144*c* plus 155) appear in *A.T.L.*, II, Plates XIV and XV; see also *S.E.G.*, X, 108.

Line 2: Ἀρχικλε̣̂[ς] *A.T.L.* The epsilon is represented by the lower part of a left-hand vertical. Since the name has Ionic lambda and line 1 includes a xi in a document that is otherwise Attic in its orthography, we should probably write Ἀρχ̣ικλῆ̣[ς].

Line 4: [ἐπρυτάνευ]ε [Ἀρχικλ]ε͂[ς] BM.

Line 5: [Ἀντικράτες] ἐ[πε]στά[τ] BM.

Line 9: χρόν̣[οι] BM. The left-hand hasta is visible.

Line 13: τὸν δέ BM.

Lines 32–37: Our version of the faint traces on the smoothed stone follows:

ΣΑΣΣΤ̣Ε̣Σ̣
.ΛΣΚ.Ε̣Τ
ΕΤΟΝ...
...Ν..Μ
..Ι....
..Ι....

Bibliography

Andokides. *Andocidis Orationes*, ed. Friedrich Blass (fourth edition, revised by C. Fuhr, Leipzig, 1913).

Aristotle. *Aristotelis Atheniensium respublica*, ed. F. G. Kenyon (Oxford, 1920).

Barron, John P. "Milesian Politics and Athenian Propaganda *c.* 460–440 B.C.," *J.H.S.*, LXXXII (1962), pp. 1–6.

———. *The Silver Coins of Samos* (London, 1966).

Bechtel, Friedrich. *Die historischen Personennamen des Griechischen bis zur Kaiserzeit* (Hildesheim, 1964).

Bengtson, Hermann. *Die Staatsverträge des Altertums*, II, *Die Verträge der griechisch-römischen Welt von 700 bis 338 v. Chr.*, in collaboration with Robert Werner (Munich and Berlin, 1962).

Bonner, Robert J., and Gertrude Smith. *The Administration of Justice from Homer to Aristotle*, I (Chicago, 1930).

Bradeen, Donald W. "The Popularity of the Athenian Empire," *Historia*, IX (1960), pp. 257–69.

———. "The Athenian Casualty Lists," *Class. Quart.*, N.S. XIX (1969), pp. 145–59.

Broneer, Oscar. "Excavations on the North Slope of the Acropolis in Athens, 1933–1934," *Hesperia*, IV (1935), pp. 109–88, especially 154–58 (on fragments of Lists 35 and 39).

Demosthenes. *Demosthenis Orationes*, 3 vols. (Oxford, 1903–1931), I and II, 1 ed. S. H. Butcher, II, 2 and III ed. W. Rennie.

Diodoros. *Diodori Bibliotheca Historica*, II, edited by Fr. Vogel (third edition, 1890; reprint Stuttgart, 1964).

Dow, Sterling. *Conventions in Editing: A Suggested Reformulation of the Leiden System* (*Greek Roman and Byzantine Scholarly Aids*, 2, Duke University, 1969).

Fornara, Charles W. "The Date of the 'Regulations for Miletus,'" *A.J.P.*, XCII (1971), pp. 473–75.

Foucart, P. "Inscription d'Éleusis du Vme siècle," *B.C.H.*, IV (1880), pp. 225–56, especially 250–51 (on D11).

Fredrich, C. (ed.) *Inscriptiones Graecae*, XII, 8, *Inscriptiones insularum maris Thracici* (Berlin, 1909).

Gomme, A. W. *A Historical Commentary on Thucydides*, I, *Introduction and Commentary on Book I* (Oxford, 1945).

———. "*IG* I^2 60 and Thucydides III 50.2," in George E. Mylonas and Doris Raymond (eds.), *Studies Presented to David Moore Robinson on His Seventieth Birthday*, II (Saint Louis, Missouri, 1953), pp. 334–39.

———, A. Andrewes, and K. J. Dover, *A Historical Commentary on Thucydides*, IV, *Books V 25–VII* (Oxford, 1970).

Haggard, Patience. *The Secretaries of the Athenian Boule in the Fifth Century B.C.* (Diss., Missouri, 1930).

Herrmann, P. "Zu den Beziehungen zwischen Athen und Milet im 5. Jahrhundert," *Klio*, LII (1970), pp. 163–73.

Hiller von Gaertringen, Friedrich (ed.). *Inscriptiones Graecae*, V, 2, *Inscriptiones Arcadiae* (Berlin, 1913).

——— (ed.). *Inscriptiones Graecae*, I, *Inscriptiones Atticae Euclidis anno anteriores* (editio minor, Berlin, 1924).

Hondius, Jacobus Johannes Ewoud *Novae Inscriptiones Atticae* (Leyden, 1925), no. II with Figs. 2 and 3 (D15).

———, (ed.). *Supplementum Epigraphicum Graecum*, III (Leyden, 1929); V (1931).

———, and A. E. Raubitschek (eds.). *Supplementum Epigraphicum Graecum*, X (Leyden, 1949).

Hopper, R. J. "Interstate Juridical Agreements in the Athenian Empire," *J.H.S.*, LXIII (1943), pp. 35–51.

Jameson, Michael H. "A Revised Text of the Decree of Themistokles from Troizen," *Hesperia*, XXXI (1962), pp. 310–15.

Kahrstedt, Ulrich. Review of Meritt, *A.F.D.*, and Meritt and West, *The Athenian Assessment of 425 B.C.*, in *Gött. gel. Anz.*, CXCVII (1935), pp. 41–54.

———. "Untersuchungen zu athenischen Behörden, II: Die Nomotheten und die Legislative in Athen," *Klio*, XXXI (1938), pp. 1–32.

Kaibel, Georg (ed.). *Inscriptiones Graecae*, XIV, *Inscriptiones Italiae et Siciliae* (Berlin, 1890).

Kirchhoff, Adolph (ed.). *Inscriptiones Graecae*, I, *Inscriptiones Atticae Euclidis anno vetustiores* (Berlin, 1873, with supplements in 1877, 1886, 1891).

Kirchner, Johannes (ed.). *Inscriptiones Graecae*, II–III, *Inscriptiones Atticae Euclidis anno posteriores* (editio minor, Berlin, from 1913).

Köhler, Ulrich. "Attische Inschriften," *Hermes*, II (1867), pp. 16–36, especially 16–18 (on *I.G.*, I², 19).

———. *Urkunden und Untersuchungen zur Geschichte des delisch-attischen Bundes* (*Abh. Ak. Berlin*, 1869, published 1870).

Koumanoudes, Stephanos A. "*Ἀττικὰ ψηφίσματα*," *Ἀθήναιον*, V (1876), pp. 74–106 and 164–91, especially 82–85 and 167 (on D11).

———. "*Ἐπιγραφαὶ ἐκ τῶν περὶ τὸ Ἀσκληπιεῖον τόπων*," *Ἀθήναιον*, VI (1877), pp. 127–48, especially 127–28 (on D11).

Lepper, F. A. "Some Rubrics in the Athenian Quota-Lists," *J.H.S.*, LXXXII (1962), pp. 25–55.

Lewis, David M. "Notes on Attic Inscriptions," *B.S.A.*, XLIX (1954), pp. 17–50.

Lipsius, Justus Hermann. *Das attische Recht und Rechtsverfahren unter Benutzung des attischen Prozesses*, von M. H. E. Meier und

G. F. Schömann, dargestellt von Justus Hermann Lipsius, III (Leipzig, 1915), especially pp. 827, n. 83, and 972 with n. 19 (on D11).

Lolling, A. "'*Ἐπιγραφικαὶ ἀνακαινώσεις*," *Δελτ. Ἀρχ.* (1891), pp. 105–108.

Mattingly, Harold B. "The Methone Decrees," *Class. Quart.*, N. S. XI (1961), pp. 154–65.

———. "The Athenian Coinage Decree," *Historia*, X (1961), pp. 148–88.

———. "The Growth of Athenian Imperialism," *Historia*, XII (1963), pp. 257–73.

———. "Athenian Imperialism and the Foundation of Brea," *Class. Quart.*, N. S. XVI (1966), pp. 172–92.

———. "Periclean Imperialism," in E. Badian (ed.), *Ancient Society and Institutions: Studies Presented to Victor Ehrenberg on his 75th Birthday* (Oxford, 1966), pp. 193–223.

———. "Athenian Finance in the Peloponnesian War," *B.C.H.*, XCII (1968), pp. 450–85.

———. "Athens and the Western Greeks: c. 500–413 B.C.," *Atti del I Convegno del Centro Internazionale di Studi Numismatici* (1967), in *Annali*, XII–XIV, *Supplemento* (1969), pp. 201–21.

———. "'Epigraphically the Twenties Are Too Late . . . ,'" *B.S.A.*, LXV (1970), pp. 129–49.

———. "Formal Dating Criteria for Fifth Century Attic Inscriptions," *Acta of the Fifth International Congress of Greek and Latin Epigraphy Cambridge 1967* (Oxford, 1971), pp. 27–33.

McGregor, Malcolm F. Review of Meiggs and Lewis, *G.H.I.*, in *Phoenix*, XXIV (1970), pp. 176–82.

Meiggs, Russell. "The Growth of Athenian Imperialism," *J.H.S.*, LXIII (1943), pp. 21–34.

———. "The Crisis of Athenian Imperialism," *H.S.C.P.*, LXVII (1963), pp. 1–36.

———. "The Dating of Fifth-Century Attic Inscriptions," *J.H.S.*, LXXXVI (1966), pp. 86–98.

———, and David Lewis. *A Selection of Greek Historical Inscriptions to the End of the Fifth Century B.C.* (Oxford, 1969).

Meisterhans, K. *Grammatik der attischen Inschriften*, third edition, edited by Eduard Schwyzer (Berlin, 1900).

Meritt, Benjamin D. "A Revision of *I.G.* I^2, 216," *A.J.A.*, XXXI (1927), pp. 180–85.

———. *Athenian Financial Documents of the Fifth Century* (*University of Michigan Studies*, Humanistic Series, XXVII, Ann Arbor, 1932).

———. "Archelaos and the Decelean War," in *Classical Studies Presented to Edward Capps on His Seventieth Birthday* (Princeton, 1936), pp. 246–52.

———. *Documents on Athenian Tribute* (Cambridge, Mass., 1937).

———. *Epigraphica Attica* (*Martin Classical Lectures*, IX, Cambridge, Mass., 1940).

———. "Notes on Attic Decrees," *Hesperia*, X (1941), pp. 301–37.

———. "Attic Inscriptions of the Fifth Century," *Hesperia*, XIV (1945), pp. 61–133.

———. "The Athenian Alliances with Rhegion and Leontinoi," *Class. Quart.*, XL (1946), pp. 85–91.

———. "Greek Inscriptions," *Hesperia*, XXI (1952), pp. 340–80.

———. "An Athenian Decree," in George E. Mylonas and Doris Raymond (eds.), *Studies Presented to David Moore Robinson on His Seventieth Birthday*, II (Saint Louis, Missouri, 1953), pp. 298–303.

———. "Athenian Covenant with Mytilene," *A.J.P.*, LXXV (1954), pp. 359–68.

———. "Athens and the Amphiktyonic League," *A.J.P.*, LXXV (1954), pp. 369–73.

———. "The Alliance Between Athens and Egesta," *B.C.H.*, LXXXVIII (1964), pp. 413–15.

———. "The Choregic Dedication of Leagros," *G.R.B.S.*, VIII (1967), pp. 45–52.

———. "The Second Athenian Tribute Assessment Period," *G.R.B.S.*, VIII (1967), pp. 121–32.

———, and Antony Andrewes, "Athens and Neapolis," *B.S.A.*, XLVI (1951), pp. 200–209.

———, and H. T. Wade-Gery, "The Dating of Documents to the Mid-Fifth Century-I," *J.H.S.*, LXXXII (1962), pp. 67–74.

———, and ———. "The Dating of Documents to the Mid-Fifth Century-II," *J.H.S.*, LXXXIII (1963), pp. 100–117.

———, ———, and Malcolm Francis McGregor, *The Athenian Tribute Lists*, I (Cambridge, Mass., 1939); II–IV (Princeton, New Jersey, 1949, 1950, 1953).

Oliver, James Henry. "The Athenian Decree Concerning Miletus in 450/49 B.C.," *T.A.P.A.*, LXVI (1935), pp. 177–98.

———. "Inscriptions from Athens," *A.J.A.*, XL (1936), pp. 460–65, especially 460–61 (frag. 2 of *I.G.*, I², 68/69 reconstructed).

Pečírka, Jan. *The Formula For the Grant of Enktesis in Attic Inscriptions* (*Acta Universitatis Carolinae Philosophica et Historica*, Monographia XV, Prague, 1966).

Piraino, Maria Teresa Manni. "Atene ed Alicie in I.G. I²20," *Kokalos*, XVI (1960), pp. 58–70.

Pittakys, K. S. *L'ancienne Athènes ou la description des antiquités d'Athènes et de ses environs* (Athens, 1835).

———. In 'Εφ. Ἀρχ. (1853), nos. 1252, 1253, 1254 (List 26).

Plutarch. *Plutarch's Lives*, with an English translation by Bernadotte Perrin, III (*The Loeb Classical Library*, London and New York, 1916).

———. *Plutarch's Moralia*, X, *771E–854D*, with an English translation by Harold North Fowler (*The Loeb Classical Library*, London and Cambridge, Mass., 1936).

Rangabé, A. R. *Antiquités Helléniques ou répertoire d'inscriptions et d'autres antiquités découvertes depuis l'affranchissement de la Grèce*, I (Athens, 1842).

Raubitschek, Antony E. "Athens and Halikyai," *T.A.P.A.*, LXXV (1944), pp. 10–14.

Schöll, R. "Athenische Fest-Commissionen," *Sitzungsb. Ak. München* (1887), pp. 1–24.

Thucydides. *Thucydidis Historiae*, ed. Henry Stuart Jones, revised by John Enoch Powell (2 vols. Oxford, 1942).

Tod, Marcus N. *A Selection of Greek Historical Inscriptions to the End of the Fifth Century B.C.*, I (Oxford, 1933; second edition, 1946).

Wade-Gery, H. T. "The Financial Decrees of Kallias (*I.G.* I², 91–92)," *J.H.S.*, LI (1931), pp. 57–85.

———. *Essays in Greek History* (Oxford, 1958).

Walbank, Michael Burke. *Athenian Proxenies of the Fifth Century B.C.* (Diss., British Columbia, 1970).

West, Allen Brown. "Prosopographical Notes on the Treaty Between Athens and Haliai," *A.J.P.*, LVI (1935), pp. 72–76.

Wilamowitz-Moellendorff, Ulrich von. *Aristoteles und Athen* (2 vols. Berlin, 1893).

Wilhelm, Adolf. *Attische Urkunden*, IV (*Sitzungsb. Ak. Wien*, CCXVII, 5, Vienna and Leipzig, 1939).

Will, E. "Notes sur les régimes politiques de Samos au Vᵉ siècle," *Rev. ét. anc.*, LXXI (1969), pp. 305–19.

Woodhead, A. G. "Greek Inscriptions," *Hesperia*, XVII (1948), pp. 54–60, especially 58–60 (on *I.G.*, I², 19 and 20).

——— (ed.). *Supplementum Epigraphicum Graecum*, XII (Leyden, 1955); XIII (1956); XIV (1957); XIX (1963); XXI (1965); XXIII (1968); XXIV (1970).

———. *The Study of Greek Inscriptions* (Cambridge, 1959; paperback 1967).

Xenophon. *Xenophontis Opera Omnia*, ed. E. C. Marchant, I, *Historia Graeca* (Oxford, 1900).

[Xenophon]. *Ἀθηναίων Πολιτεία*, in *Xenophontis Opera Omnia*, ed. E. C. Marchant, V, *Opuscula* (Oxford, 1920).

List of Inscriptions Cited and Studied

Those pages on which an inscription is the subject of special or detailed study are indicated by the use of bold-faced type.

I.G., I², 11: see D10.
12/13a: see D10.
14/15+: see D15.
16: 51n.23, **116**.
19: xi, **71–81**, 73 (photograph), 92.
20: xi, **71–81**, 74 (photograph).
22+: see D11.
26: **116–117**.
27: **117**.
28a: 43n.21, **117–118**.
29: xi, 107 (photograph), **118**.
34/35: xii, 108–110 (photograph), **118–119**.
39: see D17.
45: 43, 49.
46: **119–120**.
50+: see D18.
51: 72, 121.
52: xii, 72, 111 (photograph), **121**.
57: see D3–6.
59: 50.
60+: see D22.
65+: see D8.
66+: see D7.
68/69+: vii, xi, **82–93**, 84–87 (photographs).
70+: see *S.E.G.*, X, 84.
73: 50.
76: 38, 50, 57.
86: 72, 80, 90.
87: xii, 114 (photograph), **123–124**.
96: 102n.2.
97: **124**.
101: xii, 115 (photograph), **124**.
105: **124–125**.
106: **125**.
107: **125**.
108: **125–126**.
110: 57.
124: **126**.
125: **126**.
144+: see D23.
149: xi, **100–105**, 101 (photograph).
154: 103n.6.
155+: see D23.
280: 55.

305: **126–127.**
311: **127.**
354: 77n.9.
374: 55.
944+: 102n.2.
950: 38.
II², 43: 60.
48: 103n.6.
110: 60.
111: 49.
114: 60.
116: 60.
152: 60.
179: 43n.21, 48.
1629: 47.
1672: 47.
V, 2,357: 43n.21.
XII, 8,640: 43n.21.
XIV, 432: 43n.21.
S.E.G., X, 17: see D15.
24: 39, 41.
81: see *I.G.*, I², 68/69.
84: 103n.6, **122–123.**
XVIII, 153 (Decree of Themistokles): 92.

A.T.L., II, List 1: 45, 68, 69, **127.**
2: 68.
3: 68.
7: 77n.9.
8: 77n.9.
9: 22.
12: 14, 22.
13: 14, 22.
14: 14.
15: 14, 22.
16: 22.
20: 14.
22: 14, 128.
23: 22, 128.
25: 13, 14, 16, 17, 19, 21, 22, 23 with n.24, **127–128.**
26: vi, xi, **3–23,** 5–7 (photographs).
27: 17, 21, 23n.24.
28: 21, 23n.24.
33: 45.
34: 45.
35: 4n.5.
39: 4n.5.
A9: 14, 21, 23n.24, 42, 43, 46, 47, 57, 128.
13: 128.
D3–6: 39, 90.
7: 47, 51.
8: 38, 42, 47, 65.
10: 39, **106** and **116.**
11: vi, xi, **24–70,** 26–29 (photographs).
12: 39.
13: 65n.26.
14: 33n.19, 43.
15: xi, 50, 92, 93, **94–99,** 95 (photograph).
17: 43, 52, 67 with n.29, 68n.30, 80, 92, 97n.3.
18: 98, **120–121.**
22: xii, 112–113 (photographs), **121–122.**
23: **128–129.**